RUN *with your* HEART

How Two of Life's Losers Found a Winning Partnership

STEVEN WRIGHT

RACING POST

To Alexander ... my best pal

First published in Great Britain in 2014
By Racing Post Books, 27 Kingfisher Court, Hambridge Road,
Newbury, Berkshire RG14 5SJ

1 3 5 7 9 10 8 6 4 2

ISBN 978-1-909471-74-0

Cover designed by Jay Vincent
Text designed by J Schwartz & Co.

Printed and bound in the UK by CPI Group (UK) Ltd, Croydon, CR0 4YY

www.racingpost.com/shop

Photographs: front cover © Stephen Garnett; back cover © Joanna Prestwich

Contents

Preface

This is the story of how a rather seedy city journalist, whose mistakes led to bankruptcy, a broken marriage and the bottle, found new hope and happiness in the company of a failed racehorse.

Adelphi Warrior, a tall young thoroughbred descended from the great Nijinsky, came most unexpectedly into my life, making a childhood dream come true. Like me, he was something of a lost soul. Horses that don't succeed on the racecourse can end up in 'the paddock in the sky'.

I gave him the proud stable name Alexander and made excited plans for our future. My many falls off the crafty part-gypsy trotter, Daniel, had made me the Mr Bean of local equestrianism. Alexander, known by ladies at our livery yard as 'The Creature' because of his height and athleticism, would change all that. I couldn't wait to get home to the Yorkshire Dales from my job in Bradford to ride my horse down the country lanes and gallop him in the meadows.

Then, disaster struck. Alexander suffered a terrible injury. Would he survive, let alone gallop to victory with me over cross-country fences? Had a middle-aged hobby rider grasped too eagerly at the impossible?

This is the tale of a very ordinary bloke and his pursuit of a dream. It is dedicated to everyone who loves horses and to all of us who never stop wishing.

1

The Impossible Dream

Ears pricked, the leggy, flame-haired racehorse snorted as he eyed the line of cross-country fences. Prancing on the spot, he tossed his head impatiently urging his jockey to let him go. And moments later, I did.

Alexander leapt forward, his red mane flying and his hooves thundering as he charged towards the first log. The sweeping Yorkshire Dales countryside became a blur. I shoved my heels and bottom down in a conscious act of self-preservation as I felt a pace and athleticism I had never before experienced. A thrill of excitement swept over me.

The powerful thoroughbred ate up the ground and before I had time to think, we were springing over the log as if it wasn't there. There was no time to celebrate the moment. We were hurtling on to the next jump, another log, only bigger.

Then, without warning, disaster loomed. As we neared the obstacle, The Black Mare, pounding along just ahead of us, drifted to the right. My view of the fast-approaching fence disappeared. Suddenly, we were running out of room. The horse in front had unwittingly taken our course. It was the sort of incident that jockeys have to deal with all the time in a race. But this was not a race and I am not a jockey. Exhilaration turned to blind panic.

Then, Alexander's racing instinct kicked in. As I eased back on the reins, he darted to the inside of the other horse, giving us again a clear view of the fence. He nimbly put in a short stride and we were over. I breathed a sigh of relief and gathered myself together for the last fence in the line, a daunting ski jump. The muscular steeplechaser was warming to the occasion. Now we were powering forward in front of the mare. 'This looks challenging,' I thought.

I had no choice as my chestnut steed raced exuberantly onwards. I wrapped my legs even more tightly around him, striving for extra security as he stood off the fence. I felt the spring of his powerful flanks propelling us through the air. Landing, he was straight back into his stride, galloping away as if it was the finish of the Grand National with the winning post in sight.

'Can you stop him?' I asked myself, the fear of a painful fall looming large as we bounced along.

Surprisingly, when I rather desperately applied the brakes, they worked and slowly the pace decreased. As Alexander eased down he became even springier. He shook his head in what seemed a mix of pleasure and frustration. I felt myself shift slightly in the saddle and I thrust my heels down further. I was not going to fall off now.

And then it was over. Alexander stood still, snorting and gently quivering. I allowed myself to relax and pat his long, slim neck. 'That was bloody amazing,' I said quietly.

A couple of hours later, I sat in the pub, weary but elated, and reflected on what I had done that afternoon. It was hard to believe. I was a 52-year-old bloke from the suburbs of Leeds who had lived most of my life in the city and worked full-time for decades in an office. My sporting achievements were limited to two seasons of local Sunday league pub football nearly 30 years ago and a handful of unimpressive performances on the cricket field.

Until recently, my only riding experience was a couple of holiday treks and a few months plodding round at a riding school. The nearest I had got to jumping anything was hopping, eyes shut in terror, over a tiny woodland stream. But now I was riding an amazingly well-bred and athletic horse, whose father had finished sixth in the most famous of all Flat races, the Epsom Derby. Galloping Alexander, and jumping fences on him, was to live a childhood dream that I would have thought impossible. How had it happened?

My life had been in a complete mess and my future had looked bleak. I had struggled to put bankruptcy, a broken marriage and a drink problem behind me. Then I met Jenny, who gave me love, and the opportunity to indulge my passion for horses.

Alexander's life was also at a crossroads. He was just six years old but was already on the scrapheap. Bred to race, but physically and mentally immature, he had failed dismally. After two steeplechases his racing career was brought to an end. He was uncertain, tetchy, and too athletic for his own good. Who would want him now?

Pure chance would bring us together; two lost souls who would become soulmates. We would find happiness and new purpose – something that had seemed beyond us both – and share a success I could never have foreseen.

2

A Passion For Racing

As a boy, I loved watching sport on television. Rugby League, soccer, cricket, golf. You name it, I watched it. BBC's *Grandstand*, on a Saturday afternoon, was the highlight of my week. It started with the lunchtime *Football Focus*. In those days it was presented by Sam Leitch, a chubby-cheeked Scotsman with an impossible accent. I found him delightfully entertaining.

The rest of the afternoon featured any number of different sports. At the start of the programme, the viewer was shown a timetable of what they could watch and when. The regular visits to Lydden Hill in Kent for the bumps and bangs and slips and slides of the rallycross races fell into the must-watch bracket, the turbo-charged commentary of Murray Walker enhancing the drama.

Live Rugby League was also not to be missed. Eddie Waring's unique flat cap and whippet microphone style: 'It's an 'oop an' under' added strangely to the excitement. And then there was the horse racing. Each Saturday, *Grandstand* screened three or four races, usually from one of the bigger name courses, such as Newbury, Haydock, Ascot and Kempton. The coverage was professional and polished and the action thrilling. I found myself eagerly anticipating each race, willing the ice hockey or table tennis to finish its slot so we could get back to the racecourse. I admired the jockeys and adored the horses.

And always there was the magnificent Peter O'Sullevan. In an age of brilliant sports commentators, he was the best of the lot. His dulcet tones, ebbing and flowing in perfect tandem with the rhythm of the race, reeled you into the heart of the action.

His professionalism was unsurpassed. Even when he commentated on his own horse stealing a win in a dramatic finish, he did not betray a flicker of personal emotion. But what I really loved about O'Sullevan was the way he always informed the viewer of the fate of a horse that had stayed down after a fall. There was an uplifting lilt in his voice when he revealed that it was only winded as it finally got to its feet. On the rare occasion when the unfortunate animal was not going to get up, he told us quietly, calmly and with respect and sympathy for the horse, its connections and those of us watching. As an animal lover, that was important to me.

I had no real contact with horses as a child and there was no history of them in the family, or so I thought. My dad, Geoff, rode bareback on Shire horses at his uncle's farm in Lincolnshire when he was a lad but he never followed it up. Maureen, my mum, likes horses but they frighten her. I remember a holiday in Scotland when I was 12 or 13. My parents and I went on a trek. Mum was put on the biggest horse. In those days, health and safety wasn't the major issue it rightly is now, so there were no riding hats or tuition. You just got on the horse and set off. Mum had never sat on one. She didn't know how to ride and could not control the huge animal. It carted her up a steep bank. She survived unscathed but it was the first and last time she rode.

The only other time I can remember riding as a child was also on holiday, this time in Spain. Dad and I got on a pair of ponies and followed our Spanish guide across bare, hilly scrubland straight out of a spaghetti western. I felt like Clint Eastwood as we 'rode into town', swaggering down the dusty main street in the village.

Although I had little contact with horses, I was drawn to them. I found them fascinating and beautiful. Racehorses seemed to capture everything that was so fine about them; bravery, enthusiasm, athleticism and an ability to uplift the soul. When I watched a racehorse in action, I felt there could be nothing very wrong with the world.

I soon realised I was more attracted to the riskier side of racing. I was completely hooked on the chasers and hurdlers, galloping and jumping round a three-mile course. Flat racing left me relatively unmoved. It was over too quickly. There was not the heart-stopping drama of the thrills and spills of flying over big fences at speed.

I noted the wonderful successes of Flat-race giants of the time, such as Mill Reef, Brigadier Gerard and Nijinsky, little knowing I would one day own and ride a horse with close blood links to one of racing's greats, and I admired the balance and style of jockeys such as Lester Piggott. But what made my stomach churn and my heart pound was watching the brave jump jockeys and their equally courageous steeds.

Decades later, in middle age, I would be described as brave at my own riding level. Where that sense of adventure and need to taste danger came from, I didn't know. Nor could I pinpoint why I seemed to have a natural affinity with horses. I thought it was perhaps something to do with the gypsy blood said to flow on my mother's side of the family. It was only after I had turned 50 that I discovered that my paternal grandfather, Gordon Wright, had served in the Cavalry during the First World War and had then been asked to join the mounted section of the Rhodesian Police. He even went on to ride in point-to-point races.

I remember avidly following the jump jockeys of the early 1970s: the stylish Graham Thorner, who won the 1972 Grand National on Well To Do; Bill Smith, and Ron Barry from the north, all drive and determination; and 'The Noble Lord', amateur John Oaksey. Later, there would be the unrivalled John Francome and, in the modern era, the majestic Ruby Walsh and magnificent AP McCoy.

Then there were the horses. Some had exotic names like Sky Pink, Salmon Spray and the galloping grey Stalbridge Colonist. But I thought all of them were marvellous. For so many, the racing event that still captures the imagination is the Grand National. Families gather round the television to watch the race. Non-gamblers risk a modest once-a-year flutter. People the length and breadth of the country marvel at the occasion and gasp at the heroics of 40 horse and rider partnerships.

As a youth, the race fascinated me. I dreamed of riding in it. It was a crazy dream, but it wouldn't go away. I knew exactly how I would tackle the race. Taking my cue from the real jockeys, I decided my best plan was to hunt round the outside on the first circuit then take the shortest and bravest course up the inside the second time around and really ride. The dream always ended with me driving my mount round the elbow to snatch victory in the last few strides.

My earliest memory of the Grand National was Foinavon's race in 1967, when I was eight. The grainy black and white TV images of the blinkered and completely unfancied 100-1 shot appearing from the carnage of a big pile-up to hop over and plug on to victory are etched on the history of the race.

The following year, the winner was Red Alligator, ridden by Brian Fletcher, who would partner a very special Red to win the race two years running. In 1969 it was Highland Wedding, then Gay Trip, Specify and Well To Do. I relished each race.

The Grand National of 1973 was the greatest race ever run. It also produced a tragedy that I took personally and can still picture today.

I have always had a soft spot for front-running, bold-jumping grey steeplechasers. Desert Orchid became a national treasure with his flamboyant style. I, too, was entranced by him. And though I never saw him race, except on TV, I did twice see him in real life.

The first time was at a special open day in North Yorkshire when members of the public could go and see close up some greats from the equine world. The second occasion was also in North Yorkshire, one sunny afternoon during another holiday ride. Our guide pointed to a grey horse grazing in a distant field at the bottom of a steep hill.

'That's Desert Orchid. He's on his summer holidays,' he said.

There were other wonderful greys over the years, like Casbah and Grey Abbey. But as I hit my teens, I was smitten by a racehorse who was the most exciting and uplifting I have ever seen. I adored Grey Sombrero. He invariably set out to lead from the front and gallop his rivals into submission. Often he would just race further and further away from the opposition, fearlessly taking every fence in his flowing stride, to win.

The 1973 Grand National will always be remembered for the way the legendary Red Rum chased and caught the bold and brave Crisp in the last strides to register the first of his record-breaking three wins in the race.

But my abiding memory is of the death of Grey Sombrero. As Crisp surged clear, another horse broke away from the rest of the field and set off in pursuit. Inevitably, it was Grey Sombrero. At The Chair, the biggest fence on the course, Crisp sailed over. Grey Sombrero appeared to do the same, but he crumpled on landing, desperately tried to keep his feet and then toppled awkwardly to the ground.

It didn't look like one of the worst falls but as the field streamed past, the cameras captured him struggling to his feet. As his jockey reached for his reins, the horse hobbled forward, unable to put his weight on one of his back legs. I still remember the sick feeling I felt in my stomach and how I wept uncontrollably for him that night on learning of his fate.

For that is what horses do. They make you laugh and cry in equal measure. Sometimes the tears are of joy, not grief. You can laugh out of trepidation, as well as sheer delight. Horses touch your spirit and lift your very soul. They calm you and bring you comfort but they can also plunge you into despair. It was horses that put my life back on track and provided me with a sense of achievement and a new-found pride in myself.

As an unsure teenager, and an only child, the racehorses on the TV were a thrill and a comfort. Unable to see them in the flesh, I replicated them in a board game.

My childhood Christmas stocking always included at least one Famous Five book to be avidly read. There would also be board games, which I loved. I have fond memories of Spy Ring, where you had to break into foreign embassies to steal top-level secrets; Buccaneer, which involved plundering treasure from other pirate ships; and Alan Ball's Soccerama, where you were a football manager, aiming to guide your team from the foot of the Fourth Division to the top of the First.

The best of the lot was the Waddington's racing game, Totopoly. The board had two sides, one for training and one for the race. Training involved you picking up advantage cards the colour of your horse to use in the race, and avoiding white disadvantage cards. They had to be got rid of during the race if you wanted to win and I always did!

Each square on the board contained good or bad instructions. You hoped to land on the positive squares. There were also trainers' and vet's reports to be collected. They could be in your favour, or against you. The vet's report card you didn't want was the one that told you your horse was scratched from the race.

There were 12 horses: three blacks, Dark Warrior, Flamenco and Dorigen; three reds, Marmaduke Jinks, Leonidas II and Overcoat; three yellows, Play On, Priory Park and Knight Error and three blues, King Of Clubs, Jerome Fandor and Elton. The black horses had the most chance of winning, then the reds, then the yellows. The blues had the least chance. The blacks and the reds were trained at Walroy Stables. The yellows and the blues at Stevedon Stables. If you owned Walroy Stables, you felt like champion trainer Paul Nicholls.

At the end of training, you turned over the board and went on to the racecourse. During the race, you could manoeuvre your horse to land on advantageous coloured squares. You hoped to avoid squares with instructions like: 'Boxed in, fall back a length', or 'Swerved, go back two lengths and move to outside', while aiming for gems such as 'Flying start, go on two lengths'.

I regularly landed on 'Horse falls, throw six to remount', and would frustratingly throw everything but a six while another player went on to win the race. And how many times was I winning going round the final bend only to land on either 'Broken Rein' or 'Burst Blood Vessel'? Both signalled the end of your race. When I couldn't find anyone to play the game with, I played on my own. I was soon changing the names of the delicate, plastic horses into those of real racehorses. Marmaduke Jinks became Red Candle and Play On was soon Nereo.

Years later, when I played the game with my own children, I discovered the names of horses such as Red Rum, Rouge Autumn and Midnight Court, scribbled in blue ink in my handwriting on the inside of the battered box. By then, the horses were showing their age. Many of their fragile, plastic legs, and the heads of the jockeys, had been accidentally snapped off over the years. It didn't stop us having hours of fun.

My favourite was one of the red horses, Number 5, Leonidas II. I always hoped to draw him out in the deal at the start of the game that decided which horses you got to race with. More often than not, when I had him Leonidas II would defy the odds and beat the black horses. Twenty five years on, with a headless jockey and without his front legs, Leonidas II was still winning for me. It never crossed my mind that one day I would have my own real-life red racehorse and jump him over real fences.

A black horse would first come into my life, very beautiful and very real.

3

I Get Knocked Down

These days, I live in the countryside and I slipped easily into the rural way of life. But until my mid-forties, I was a city boy. Born in Leeds, I was brought up in the suburbs of Cross Gates and Whitkirk on the eastern side of the city. They were pleasant and middle class.

For the first years of my life, I lived with my parents in a modest, brick-built semi-detached house on a close-knit, horseshoe-shaped street. We were less than a goal kick away from the local pub and I would spend many happy hours playing wall ball against the back of its brick garage.

Our home was half a mile from the Vickers Barnbow factory and a common sound in my childhood was the distant roar of the Chieftain tanks as they were tested. I could also hear the trains thundering past on the York to Leeds line close by.

Living near to the buzz and furore of people getting from A to B has been a theme of my life. I have lived under a flight path close to an airport, in a flat overlooking a railway station and on busy main roads. Rather than a nuisance, I found such locations comforting and reassuring, perhaps because I was an only child and the noise of people going about their lives gave me a sense of security. Even today, our cottage sits right on a village's busy main street but now the sound is less of a comfort and more an unnoticed backdrop.

I always loved to escape to the countryside and the seaside. The Yorkshire Dales, Scotland and Northumberland remain my favourite haunts. But my home was the city, whether it was Leeds, or Sheffield, where I spent the first nine years of my working life. I felt comfortable surrounded by human life and all that goes with it.

In my mid-teens, I made up my mind to be a journalist. Mum and dad warned that it was not a well-paid career but supported my decision.

My teachers were bewildered. I went to John Smeaton High School two years after it had opened and I was the first pupil to express an interest in journalism. The careers staff tried to steer me towards a safe and secure job, like banking, insurance, or the civil service, all of which left me cold.

I got myself an advisory interview at the respected *Yorkshire Post* that convinced me I had made the right choice. I remain grateful to Mr Slater, a teacher at the school, who put me on the spot in a mock interview in which he played the role of an editor, even though he knew nothing about newspapers. It was a big help when I began attending the real thing.

However getting a job proved harder than I had bargained for. I wrote to dozens of papers across Yorkshire. None were recruiting trainee journalists. I got a couple of weeks' work experience with the weekly *Dewsbury Reporter*. But again, no job.

It was then that my innate tenacity and perseverance came to the fore, qualities I would need in abundance when my life began collapsing around me years later, and again when horse riding became my passion.

The Sheffield Star was an evening paper of some repute and significant sales. In 1977 it advertised two trainee reporter vacancies. A couple of hundred would-be newshounds were vying for the posts. They whittled us down to a final six. I later learned that they could not decide between three of us but I was the outsider. The weeks had dragged by. I was anxious to know my fate and equally determined to land the job. The deputy editor told me later that, after the umpteenth call from me to ask if they had made up their minds, he declared: 'That Steve Wright is making my life hell. Sign him up!'

So began almost a decade of provincial daily news reporting. I learned much, both from my first news editor, Dave Mastin, who I feared and respected in equal measure, and my colleagues, many of whom were among the most outstanding journalists I have come across in more than 30 years in the business. I grew as a journalist and earned respect and in 1986 found myself head-hunted by a news agency working for the nationals.

My time in Sheffield was a happy one. I made many close and trusted friends and had a busy social life in a lively city. While there, I met my wife. She came to *The Star* on work experience. The newsdesk landed her with me and we ended up going out together. I proposed marriage within days. She agreed but told me to ask her again in a year. It took many more years to get anywhere near the church. By then, I was back in Leeds.

We had one false start, calling off the wedding when the reception was booked and the invitations had gone out. Instead of flying out to Italy for my honeymoon, I packed my suitcase and caught a train to Bridlington on the East Yorkshire coast on my own. I arrived at the resort with no accommodation booked and wandered around the streets near the harbour with my case, looking for a place to stay. I stumbled upon a modest guest house with vacancies. It was called the Leeds Hotel, which seemed appropriate, and I booked in. I was the only resident but it suited me at the time.

The week passed in a haze of booze, fags and sentimental music. I returned to Leeds with my mind wiped clean and determined to put my life back in order. But within months my wife and I had got back together. She wanted to try again and I agreed, though my family was less convinced. In September, 1991, we married at our local church. Just over a year later our daughter, Emma, was born. Sophie and Ben followed.

It was during the first year of my marriage, and now in my thirties, that I found a riding school down the road and started going there on Saturday mornings. The first horse I rode was a gentle giant called Ginger. When I turned up for my second lesson, I was told I was riding Nessie. She was a stubborn, temperamental mare who no-one was keen on. She would either dig in her toes and refuse to budge or bugger off without warning.

But I struck up a relationship with her that developed after a comical fall I had the first time I rode her. We were plodding slowly round the outdoor school when she tripped over her feet. Her head came down and I slid along her neck and rolled to the ground. Nessie looked down triumphantly at me. Her expression changed when I clambered back on, and we got on like a house on fire after that. I always asked to ride her and she seemed pleased to see me. The lessons came to an end after Emma was born and I had other responsibilities. I hadn't learned many riding skills but I did have great fun.

As the years went by, my marriage disintegrated. I think my wife and I are decent people, but we saw things differently and the longer we were together the further apart we grew and the more we argued. The end of the relationship was hastened by my ever-growing financial difficulties. Like my drinking, they were to spiral out of control and lead me to the brink of disaster.

I have always liked a drink. I was quite a late starter and must have been 17 when I went to the Brown Cow in Whitkirk with my best mate, Rick Potter. We started out drinking Tetley's bitter or mild, washed down with a few Southern Comforts.

I remember the first time I got home drunk. It was after closing time and Mum and Dad had gone to bed. They must have been listening out anxiously for my safe return. They were not to be disappointed. After fumbling with my key, I managed to open the front door and, with great deliberation, close it behind me. I then stood swaying in the hall until I felt capable of sitting down to take off my shoes. Inevitably, I lost my balance and crashed backwards into the metal central heating radiator, making it reverberate with a racket that could have woken the dead. Instead, it brought my parents dashing to the top of the stairs. Safe to say, they weren't impressed.

The booze got me into a few scrapes over the years. I once insulted the owner of a posh hotel where I was staying in Lytham St

Annes on the Lancashire coast during a row over Yorkshire cricket legend Geoff Boycott, and then fell off my bar stool. The staff had a good laugh at my expense as they carried me up to my room. The Red Rose had the last word on that particular skirmish.

Though I enjoyed booze, and drank more than was good for me, I was never an alcoholic. I didn't need it when I woke up in the morning and I could go for weeks without touching it. But by the mid to late 1990s, it was becoming a crook to hold on to. As my life became more miserable and chaotic, the drink became an escape.

As a journalist, drink was part of the job. If you wanted to get the best stories, you had to go to the pub and talk to people. I did that regularly for years. Then, when things got tough, I turned to alcohol.

In 1986, I became a freelance journalist with a news agency based in Bradford. It worked almost exclusively for the national papers and was one of the most respected agencies in the north. I worked bloody hard but it was a great life. We were doing the best stories better than just about anybody else and playing as hard as we worked.

The agency had made good money rolling out the exclusives during the Yorkshire Ripper inquiry. But by the 1990s, the bubble had burst. The national papers were much more reluctant to pay the freelances. There were suddenly lots of us out there as the papers axed reporters. That meant they could let us all compete against each other without having to pay us all.

As the new millennium dawned, the boss of the agency, his health failing and his earnings dwindling, decided it was time to retire. He wanted me to take over. I thought long and hard about his business proposal and sought the advice of many friends and colleagues. They all said the same thing, don't do it. The price was high and I didn't have the money to pay for a cheap holiday, let alone a business. I was in serious debt. Loans and credit cards were piling up and any spare money I had was going on the booze.

To buy the business, I needed a £20,000 bank loan, if I could find the cash to match it. The only way I could do that was to ask my parents to dig into their savings. They were uncomfortable about the deal. They sensed, rightly, that something didn't add up. But they could see how much I wanted it, so they supported me with hard cash.

In the end, I let my heart overrule the niggling doubts in my head, and I did the deal. It was the biggest mistake of my life and cost me my marriage, my home, and my car, not to mention my happiness, and almost my sanity. More importantly, there was a cost for those whom I loved. My parents, who had their savings torn away and their peace of mind shattered, and my children, who saw their parents at war and their dad leave home.

Having taken on the business, I moved into modest rented premises 100 yards down the street from the old office. I set out with great intentions, making weekly trips to the office supply store and determined to do things right. I found two members of staff, one to help me with the news stories and one to write features.

The deal had been to pay most of the purchase price upfront and the rest in monthly instalments, depreciating over three years. It didn't take long to realise that the burden of those payments, allied to the wages for my two staff, office rent and tax demands, far outweighed what I was earning. It didn't help that I had to spend half my time earning money and the other half chasing what I was owed, and often not getting it.

After just a few months, I was forced to slash my wage bill by letting my feature writer go. But things didn't improve. The further it went, the more the business struggled, and the worse my financial position got. I had to let my other member of staff go, leaving just myself and my wife, but the downward spiral continued. I was faced with selling our neat little semi-detached house on a quiet, leafy street. It was nothing special but it was our home, which we had worked hard for, and it hurt to leave.

At the same time, I gave up the office and rented a large detached bungalow, which was big enough for a decent-sized room to be used as my office, combining home and work. But the rent matched the size of the property, and the garden was huge. In the summer, it took most of a back-breaking Sunday every week to keep on top of it.

Despite all my efforts to make ends meet, I was doomed to fail. I knew the end was near the day a burly man came to the house to repossess my blue Citroen Xsara estate car because I had got so far behind with the repayments. I was so proud of that car. I felt a terrible emptiness and a sense of total failure as I watched it disappear out of sight down the road.

By December 2002, having unsuccessfully tried to stave off financial disaster, and feeling crushed, I was forced to endure the embarrassment of going to Bradford County Court and declaring myself bankrupt. It was a humiliating low point in my life.

It now seems ironic that bankruptcy gave me the chance to move forward. I felt too down to appreciate it at the time, though I was determined to somehow make a new start.

In fact, I have never looked back from that point, but it took years to rebuild the shattered shell I had become.

The first step was to put behind me the uncertainty of freelancing. By the summer of 2003, I had got myself the security of a job with the *Telegraph & Argus* in Bradford. After three months, I was appointed crime reporter.

I was starting to put back together the pieces of my life but the greatest and most significant changes were yet to come.

4

She's The One

In 2002, while I was taking to the bottle to drown my woes, Jenny Loweth began a new life in the Yorkshire Dales. Within two years our paths would cross, transforming my life and bringing Alexander into it.

Jenny bought a small cottage on the main street in a village near Skipton. Despite the constant swish and roar of traffic past its traditional white front door, it was a haven and the pretty walled garden at the back was comparatively peaceful.

It lashed down with rain on the removal date in early August. The River Aire, flowing a minute's walk away, burst its banks and the removal lorry got stuck, appropriately enough, in Pool, near Otley.

When the weather cleared, Jenny spent the late summer days walking her lurcher by the river and along the canal towpath.

She felt a sense of immediate belonging in the Yorkshire Dales. Its dry stone walls, fast bubbling water and rolling hills evoked childhood memories of the Lake District where she grew up.

After settling into the cottage, she prepared to make a significant purchase. She had promised to buy a horse for her teenage daughter, Esme.

Jenny's early years were spent falling off a succession of ponies at Mr Dawson's riding school. Mr Dawson was small, weathered and wiry, with bow-legs, moulded by decades of equestrian commitment. His rotund and recalcitrant ponies had sensible names, like Bob, Bessie and Barney.

Later, Jenny acquired her own pony, an elderly, ewe-necked bay with very definite ideas about what he did, and did not, want to do. With a mediocre mount, no transport and little real riding ability, her route to showjumping success was always going to be challenging. When she stopped riding at 18 to go to college, she was left with a handful of rosettes for mounted games and a first prize for a fancy-dress contest in which she dressed her younger sister, Vanessa, and her pony as a horseradish. Jenny wanted better for Esme. The new horse would be a winner. But first she had to find it.

Soon after moving into her new home, she visited a local livery yard, set high on the hillside overlooking the village. The manager, Pat Fitton, greeted her, paintbrush in hand. She was smartening up the yard's enormous six-horse wagon with her customary vigour and enthusiasm. Pat showed her round tidy rows of indoor stables and Jenny was impressed by the mechanical horse walker and the all-weather schooling arena. She asked Pat to help her find her winning horse but she refused, saying: 'Choosing 'osses for other folk is asking for trouble.'

Back in the village, Jenny crossed the busy main street to the newsagents for a copy of *The Farmers Guardian*. And there she was. 'Black Mare. 15.3hh. Just over from Ireland.'

The dealer's yard, near Preston, was neat and compact. The Black Mare, tacked up and newly shod, was placid and gentle. Jenny rode her in the school and Esme took her a little way up the lane. Esme was immediately sure this was the horse for her, but Jenny urged caution.

'We mustn't buy the first horse we look at,' she insisted as they drove away. Halfway home, she stopped the car and rang and bought her. We still have the sales docket, written on a worn and folded sheet of lined exercise paper. 'Recipt for Black Mare. 5 year old. to be sound. Joust backed. Riding quite. No voices at all, stable or other wise. £2,000 with tack.'

'Isn't she the most beautiful horse in all the world?' Jenny said to Pat.

Pat, who had spotted the ringworm, spirited the newcomer off to a loose box on the end of the row, where she surreptitiously daubed the offending bald patch with Sudocrem.

The mare had no name and, although she plays an important role in my journey with horses, she will remain 'The Black Mare'.

I first met Jenny at Leeds Crown Court. She was covering cases there for the *Telegraph & Argus* but, as the paper's crime reporter, I wanted a hand in the big murder trials. That meant, as far as I was concerned, doing the best parts of the cases, the beginning and the end, while Jenny filled in with what she crossly termed the 'girlie bits' in between. It created a bitter rivalry between us for the front page stories and it didn't help in developing a friendly relationship.

We saw one another regularly in the Crown Court press room but attraction was far from instantaneous, on either side. All I saw was a stressy rival wanting to take my stories. By then, my job and the booze were my escape routes. I was keen to throw myself into the court stories but even keener to get to the pub with my pals. I was a smoker then and sat in the press room, wreathed in blue vapour, dourly phoning my copy to the office before joining other male hacks for a few pints. Jenny thought I was arrogant and rather seedy.

In those days, the newspaper group held a lavish Christmas party, with a live band, buffet and speech from the management. Everybody turned up and the drink flowed, which suited me fine. In December 2004, the bash was held at Valley Parade, the football stadium rebuilt after the Bradford City fire disaster.

Jenny, who had been persuaded at the last minute to attend, arrived on a coach from Skipton with journalists from the local weekly paper, the *Craven Herald*. They were all sitting round a large circular table, having a good time. Jenny was clearly enjoying herself. She looked happy and was laughing a lot. For the first time, I was struck by how attractive she was. She was slim, with a bewitching smile and her eyes danced and sparkled. I had always been too engrossed in my work and my unhappiness to notice before. I went to the bar and as I returned with my drink, I stopped to exchange pleasantries. It was probably the first time I had been nice to her.

I returned to the *Telegraph & Argus* table. After a few minutes my colleagues got up to dance. I stayed seated and soon after, I saw Jenny approaching. She asked if she could join me and I was delighted to say yes. We began talking and it seemed like we had been friends for years. We soon found we had something in common, a love of horses. Jenny told me she owned three. In contrast, I hadn't been near one in years but I wanted to hear everything about hers. She told me all about The Black Mare, and her latest equine acquisitions – a two-year-old gypsy trotter called Daniel, and his younger half-brother, Baby Horse.

'I would love to see them,' I told her. But there didn't seem to be any chance of that.

By the end of the evening we had become very close and it was with great regret that I watched her leave with her friends from the *Herald*.

A couple of days later my phone rang at work. It was Jenny, and she was calling to apologise for being over-friendly. Before she could get off the phone I had asked to see her again. I knew it was wrong, but I could not help myself. I was fascinated by her. To my surprise and delight, she reluctantly agreed.

My marriage had been effectively over for some time but I was still living at the marital home. It was a miserable existence for all of us, but there seemed no alternative. I finally plucked up the courage to leave one Sunday morning early in January 2005. The night before there had been another terrible row. I had left the house in floods of tears and sought comfort from my cousin, who lived up the road.

I realised that I just could not live like that any longer. So the next morning I packed my few belongings into my car and drove away. Hugging and saying goodbye to my children, and then turning my back and tearing myself away from them, was the toughest and most heartbreaking thing I have had to do in my life.

But in the long-term it was the right thing, for everybody's sake. None of us could have carried on living the way we were. I have always been there for my children and I am immensely proud of them. We remain close and it is always lovely to see them.

I had no clear idea about what would happen next. I drove to the office and sought advice from a colleague who was on duty. I then phoned a friend who immediately took me in as a temporary guest at his house in Bingley. He put me up for a couple of months while I got my head straight. We enjoyed relaxing evenings drinking wine and listening to classical rock music. It was a great bolthole that allowed me to get back on my feet and I shall always be grateful to him. When I left he sent me on my way with words of support and a collection of classic cutlery.

I rented a place of my own, a tall, old terraced house in Bingley with a cellar and a back yard. It was basic and relatively expensive but it was comfortable and it gave me the chance both to have my children to stay and to be alone and listen to my music with a beer as I rebuilt myself.

I continued to see Jenny. Our relationship in the first few months was fragile. We brought a lot of emotional baggage to it and the practicalities were challenging. But I had found a new happiness and security, and I knew she was the one. As time passed, we became more settled and trusting and both of us began to realise how much we cared for and depended on each other.

In the late spring of 2006, I gave up the rented house and moved in with her.

5

Thrills And Spills

My reintroduction to riding after 12 years was on The Black Mare. I had been happy to announce, to anyone who asked, that I could ride. And I honestly believed what I said. I would soon learn that perching as a passenger on the back of a placid riding school horse was a whole lot different from controlling an athletic and forward going part-thoroughbred.

Not that The Black Mare had always been athletic and forward going. Back in 2002, as she was settling into her new home, Pat Fitton would say: 'That's been brought up in a shit-hole,' relating how the mare would lie herself luxuriously down on her mound of fresh straw before Pat even had the chance to fork it round the stable for her.

That autumn, work began to get her fit, coupled with the exciting task of teaching her to jump. Jenny rode her out with her new friends, Keith Rosier and Nicola Binns, who walked their horses for miles in the mornings to keep them eventing and racing fit.

Keith, a former amateur jockey, has become my close friend and he plays his part in Alexander's story.

The Black Mare would lag further and further behind until the others had marched off out of sight. Coming back up the steep, winding hill from the village, she trailed dismally at the rear, arriving back at the yard after Keith and Nicola had untacked their horses, rugged them up and made a coffee. Often, Jenny felt so sorry for her that she dismounted and led her the last few hundred yards.

Then, a visit from the equine dentist revealed that the mare was aged four, not five.

'It's tired. It's still growing,' Pat said.

'When will it not be tired?' Jenny would ask.

'When it stops growing,' was the response.

The Black Mare looked the same size to Jenny. It seemed she would be growing forever. And, consequently, tired. A birthday card from Nicola in those early years shows a black horse lying on a cosy straw bed under a blue flowered counterpane. She has curlers in her mane and tail. Her rider, bringing her a steaming cup of morning tea, is saying: 'About the show today?'

But The Black Mare grew into a fit, enthusiastic and powerful horse. Jenny first allowed me to take her into the school at the livery yard. All went well at first as we walked and then trotted around the perimeter. But then I got ahead of myself. I thought that things were going so well we could move up to a canter. It was a disaster. As the mare's speed increased, my control of her decreased and the inevitable happened. We careered round a corner and ploughed up the middle of the school. With the boundary fence looming, the mare screeched to a halt and I flew over her shoulder, landing in the sand. She peered contemptuously down at me as Jenny looked on in dismay. It was the first of many falls I was to have in the following months and years.

Jenny decided it was safer for me to ride beyond the confined space of the school. She took me to the field opposite the yard and we ambled through a gate and down a track. The hack was gentle and trouble-free until we turned for home. Jenny, who was on foot, advised that the mare could get quite frisky at this point, but if she ran down the winding path, she would stop at the next gate. I was instructed to shorten my reins, put my heels down and sit up straight, riding skills that I struggled to put into practice for years. True to Jenny's word, the mare took off, pelted down the path and pulled up with her head over the gate. It was hair-raising but exciting and a taste of things to come.

News of my lack of control and potential for spills brought out a crowd of interested onlookers when Jenny and I hacked out together for the first time. Her dilemma was whether to put me on the fit and powerful mare while she rode the young Daniel, or to have the safe team of her and the mare and the lethal combination of me and Daniel. She went for the first option.

We ventured back down the track opposite the stables and again the ride went smoothly, until the end. Jenny dismounted from a well-behaved Daniel at the top of the hill, next to the final gate. She said I could steadily canter The Black Mare back up the track towards her.

'Don't go too far, or too fast,' I was told.

But my steady canter quickly became a gallop. Great splashes of water and clods of mud were hurled up in the air by the flying hooves as we rapidly advanced. The dark greatcoat I rather oddly wore, giving me the Cossack look, flapped wildly in the sheer momentum of the mare's magnificently untamed approach. Jenny described the vision of the flying black horse and the cloaked, dark, hunched figure as like *The Devil Rides Out*. I was proud of how I stuck on as we 'motorbiked' round a sharp corner and charged up the final hill towards a remarkably unconcerned Daniel. The crowd at the yard stared across at the unfolding drama, although some people said afterwards they dared not look. Others expressed surprise at how I managed to pull up in one piece.

Now it was time to get on Daniel. There was something special about my first encounter with him. It was in late January 2005 that our eyes met through the steel bars that formed part of his stable in the large, airy barn at the livery yard. Jenny had bought him seven months before from a dealer for £550 and he had already built up a menacing reputation at the stables. The part-gypsy trotter, a dark chocolate colour with a big white face, had kicked, bitten and fought with the farriers. You didn't go into his stable when he was eating, which was often, and you certainly didn't turn your back on him.

As I looked cautiously into his stable, my gaze was met by a pair of deep, black, unblinking eyes, searching out my very soul. I could see wariness in them, and anger, and a great intelligence. But there was something else. An instant, strange trust and affection. In that moment of meeting, I realised that here was the four-legged friend I had never had.

Others at the livery yard found Daniel harder to love. Exasperated shouts of 'Dan-yal' rang out from the staff at mucking out time as he thrust his heavy, bullock-like head into rows of brushes and forks left in the aisle and sent them clattering on to the concrete floor. He snapped the chain across the entrance to his box to steal another horse's breakfast and smashed the manger rack in his stable in his eagerness to devour his own food.

Like a deprived child sent to an expensive boarding school, Daniel had a huge chip on his shoulder. At the merest hint of any slight, his bog-brush mane bristled with resentment and his boot-button eyes glared with a smouldering fury.

If the challenge of riding The Black Mare was to control her pace and power, Daniel demanded very different qualities. Where she was keen to gallop freely and to tackle any jumping obstacle, he needed plenty of persuasion to do anything much. The only time he showed any real enthusiasm was when it came to getting rid of his rider, usually me. I clocked up double figures for the number of falls I had in the first year.

It was almost always the same scene, played in four parts: One – Daniel trots or canters amicably along; Two – Daniel is, or pretends to be, frightened by something lurking in the undergrowth; Three – Daniel shies violently, spins round and runs back the opposite way; Four – I find I have no horse beneath me and chase after Daniel on foot.

I can't remember the first fall I had from Daniel and I quickly lost count, but often they involved something furry or feathered. Having been tethered near the motorway in Bradford for the early part of his life, Daniel found it difficult to adapt to the countryside. Cattle and sheep took on the appearance of terrifying aliens to him. His first close encounter of the herd kind left him transfixed with horror. His bog-brush mane stood on end, his eyes bulged in sheer disbelief and his ears strained forward in alarm. He shot past the horse he was with and then planted himself, snorting, in the road when he realised he was left to face the menace on his own.

One of the first falls I had from Daniel was while learning to jump in a meadow at the livery yard. As we approached the red and white showjumping poles, he noticed he had an audience. Just yards away, and directly in line with the fence, half a dozen calves were peering at him from over a stone wall. Poor Daniel was horrified. In his alarm, he took a huge leap over the fence, turned sharp left and ran in the opposite direction to escape. It was too much for my flimsy riding skills and I hit the deck hard. Gingerly, I picked myself up to see Daniel disappearing into the distance with his reins and stirrups flapping. It was to become a familiar sight.

Over time, Daniel's terror of large farm animals abated but he would still rather meet a giant cement-mixing lorry in the road than a single loose sheep. His biggest fear was of birds, especially those that flew out of the undergrowth as he trundled innocently along. The pheasant season was never a good time to take Daniel into the fields. Inevitably, a bird would suddenly emerge, flapping wildly and calling raucously, and fly past his nose. Just as suddenly, Daniel would perform his practised spin and go act. The result was always the same.

David Horton, for many years head groom on the nearby Coniston Estate, once said that the first equestrian lesson I learned was how to stick on Daniel. There have been some classic examples. Nobody likes falling off and I was determined to stay in the saddle if I could.

Early on in our partnership, we had a day out cross-country jumping at Craven Country Ride. Known locally as Coates's, because it is run by former amateur jockey David Coates and his family, Craven Country Ride is probably our favourite place to go. David holds seasonal trail rides and hosts cross-country events there and it is open for much of the year for riders to practise jumping everything from event fences to tiny logs or to simply enjoy a gentle canter round. We have taken full advantage over the years of this wonderful facility on our doorstep.

Although I have good natural balance, I was too easily dislodged from the saddle, especially when Daniel got worried and over-jumped. Many times I was pitched up round his neck. When that happened, Daniel kept on running, often from side to side. If you were going, he preferred to help you on your way rather than back into the saddle. This time, I ended up with my legs flailing and my arms wrapped round his neck as if in a lover's embrace. He carried on cantering and I slid round until I found myself gazing up into his eyes. Whatever my expression, it was not one of love at that moment. How I managed to clamber back into the saddle and stop him I will never know.

Another time, he unbalanced me in the cross-country field at home. In what was by then time-honoured tradition, I clung round his neck. As Daniel increased his speed, I found myself first dangling from the left side of him, then from the right side. Again, I survived. It was the nearest I will ever come to stunt riding.

Despite my ups and downs I was having a wonderful time with the horses. On the one hand, they had brought a soothing peace and serenity to my life. But they had also invigorated me and given me a new energy and purpose that uplifted me. I felt I was in a much better place.

While Daniel and I may not have been the most accomplished horse and rider partnership, we soon became one of the most entertaining. We began to get a reputation, not as the team to beat but as the one to keep a close eye on, because whenever we were in the arena something dramatic was almost certain to happen.

6

Jump

The day I won my first rosette in competition will live with me forever, not just for the proud success but for the dramatic way in which it was achieved.

It was at Silsden Riding Club Show in June 2007. I teamed up with teenager Natasha Binns, who now has a career with racehorses in Australia, and her speedy Welsh ex-trekking pony, Captain, for the Pairs class.

We decided that Natasha would go first round the showjumping course, to give us a fighting chance, while Daniel and I would attempt to consolidate when it came to our turn. True to form, Natasha and Captain jumped a very fast clear round and the pair screeched to a halt next to us to hand over the whip, baton-style. Despite Daniel's concerned expression as Captain motored towards us, we completed the handover without dropping the whip. I gave Daniel a couple of lusty kicks. He burst into a pedestrian trot and warily pottered towards the first fence. Two strides out, he dug in his toes and stopped.

Furious with him and myself, I swung him round, delivered a couple more hearty boots and he hopped reluctantly over. We were on our way, in our own time, but on our way. As we progressed, Daniel, realising he had an audience, began to warm to his task. We got over the next four jumps at a brisk trot and turned across the centre of the arena towards the sixth fence, stripy with a spread, and looking extremely large to me. Clearly, it was just as unattractive to Daniel, who whipped away in consternation.

Gathering myself together, I turned Daniel round and faced what I felt would be inevitable disaster. I kicked like mad and hung on for dear life. 'Come on, Dan!' I shouted. Daniel, terrified, ballooned our giant jump and I found myself clinging round his neck in desperation. The spectators audibly gasped, expecting me to hit the deck at any moment. But, in the words of the popular Monty Python cricket sketch: 'Of course, I was used to it by then!'

Defying gravity, I somehow shuffled myself back into the saddle as Daniel unforgivingly trundled on. Cue more gasps from the watchers, who were getting their best entertainment of the day. Still completely unbalanced, I managed to steer Daniel round the corner and booted him into the next obstacle. To his credit, he obliged, hopping over and, picking up the excitement and enthusiastic encouragement of the crowd, bursting into a canter to hurdle the last couple of fences. We surged through the finish to cheers and applause. It would not be the last time we would get sympathetic support for being the unorthodox underdogs.

Natasha, who would have won easily with a half-decent combination alongside her, was generous in her praise of our efforts as we walked out to the collecting ring and prepared for our fate. There were six pairs in the contest, with rosettes to fourth. I was sure we were getting the wooden spoon. The winners were called back into the ring, followed by the second and third placed pairs. Just one to go.

'In fourth place,' said the announcer, 'Is Steve Wright and Natasha Binns.'

I was grinning from ear to ear. The cheers and 'well dones' rang out as we lined up and received our rosettes. I leaned over and hugged Natasha, after all, it was down to her. But, at the same time, I was proud of Daniel and proud of myself. And Daniel was clearly very proud of himself. He seemed to grow in stature and visibly milked the acclaim. It was a modest achievement but it was the start of better things to come, and a wonderful moment.

There is always a challenge for a novice rider like myself, whether out competing or caring for the horses at home. I am not very practical, and the tack, especially the seemingly endless pieces of the bridle, has long been a mystery to me. Even now, I struggle to tie up the horses' haynets correctly. When I took the children on a boating holiday on the Norfolk Broads, we had to leave our moorings before breakfast one morning because my knot had slipped and our boat had drifted sideways, blocking the path of any craft coming in or out of the dyke. Left to my own devices in the stable, I can create mayhem and confusion. I was once caught trying to work out what was wrong as The Black Mare wore her saddle back to front.

I unwittingly devised a quick and efficient way to untack Daniel. It involved mistakenly undoing the bridle cheekpieces, thus allowing the bit to fall off and the whole bridle to be easily removed from his head. Putting the bridle on proved similarly troublesome. A disbelieving Esme came to my rescue when I put the reins over Daniel's head and allowed the rest of the bridle to fall to the floor in a tangled heap.

When I realised that my riding left a lot to be desired, I worked desperately hard to improve it. Not being able to afford many lessons, I did much of my learning by watching more competent riders. I spent hours seated on the bench overlooking the outdoor school watching them ride. I studied their balance, their leg position, the straightness of their backs and the way they used their hands, their seats and their upper body. Then I tried to take what I had learned and put it into practice.

It seemed to take forever, yet slowly but surely I noticed a difference. The falls got fewer. The 'washing line' reins gradually shortened. I was complemented on my soft hands and my balance. But the strength and security of my seat and, particularly, my lower leg was still a major problem. For many years it was, almost literally, my Achilles heel. A weak lower leg means two things, a susceptibility to falling off and an inability to drive a horse forward when it doesn't want to go. It added to my challenge of trying to prevent Daniel from stopping at his fences.

The young Daniel was nervous about jumping, whether he was faced with garishly decorated showjumps or scary cross-country logs. I was a rookie rider – unstylish, weak in the leg and very rough round the edges. As a combination, we weren't going to prosper quickly.

Our first public elimination came at Ilkley Horse Show, held every month in the summer. I decided, more than a little ambitiously, to have a go at a class in the main arena. Having been announced on the public address system, Daniel and I set off positively, hopping over the first three obstacles. We have a professional photo at home showing us clearing the third. Seconds later, disaster struck. Daniel took a strong dislike to the brightly coloured yellow and white spread poles at the fourth fence. Three times I presented him at it. Three times he refused to jump it. That was it. Elimination.

I had given Daniel the competing name of In Denial. It was Keith's idea because it was an anagram of the horse's name. But I felt it suited him in other ways. You could almost hear the stubborn Daniel, at yet another refusal, saying: 'I deny I have seen that fence before – I deny I want to jump that fence.'

It was good to have had a go at such a challenging course but it was a disappointment not to complete and it showed me there was still a lot of work to do on those lower legs.

Even when I persuaded Daniel to jump against his wishes, there could be problems. When I tried to take him off the end of a 2ft cross-country drop, he was horrified. He refused to go near it at first. Eventually, I got him to step up to the edge, where he determinedly dug in his toes. I kept kicking and shoving with my legs but made the mistake of leaning forward with my body to try to urge him on. Suddenly, from a standstill and in terror, Daniel launched himself into space. The dramatic forward movement hurled me over his shoulder. I bounced twice and landed in a crumpled heap as Daniel naughtily galloped off up the hill to the top of the field.

Daniel never minded water jumps, he seemed to enjoy paddling. But logs brought out the worst in him. We were convinced he thought the small gnarled ones were crocodiles out to bite his legs. He would trot or canter towards them but, just when I thought he was going to leap over, he would violently duck out the side, leaving me clinging on desperately.

We hunted for a solution to his cross-country phobia – and hunting would provide the answer.

7

The Hunter

Hunting was just about the last thing I would ever have expected to do. The Black Mare, with Esme, was the first in the family to get involved, trotting to the Boxing Day hunt meet in the village. The horse looked very smart, with her plaited mane and oiled hooves, as she joined the cavalcade setting off from the green. The streets were lined with enthusiastic crowds, cheering and clapping. Small children stroked the hounds and the horses on the green, and riders and their mounts were festively decorated with tinsel, golden bells, red bows and antlers.

The mare joined the hunt on several occasions that winter, leaping ditches and charging across the bleak Dales countryside to return, covered in mud, in the late afternoon.

Hunting animals had been made illegal and our local hunt followed drag trails, where the hounds pick up a scent path laid down by hunt members on foot. The only animals I ever saw while out hunting were the hounds and the horses. I wouldn't have done it otherwise.

I didn't seek out the hunt. It found me. People at our livery yard had been saying for a while that Daniel would make a good hunter. Jenny thought that I would love it. Such suggestions went in one ear and out the other. I didn't consider Daniel and I to be hunting types. I thought we would be well out of our comfort zone.

One autumnal morning, Daniel and I were invited on a long hack out from the yard. Among the small riding party were two stalwarts and officials of the local hunt, who kept their impressive and powerful big horses at the yard. We trekked for seven or eight miles across some tough terrain, with plenty of trotting and cantering. Little Daniel, who was still only four, doggedly kept up in good style, impressing our riding companions. Later, in the pub, they suggested we went along to the Newcomers meet the following weekend.

The Newcomers meet, at the beginning of the season, gives hunting virgins like me the chance to ride shoulder to shoulder with the scarlet-jacketed huntsmen, or at least to follow on their coat-tails. It is a cardinal sin to overtake the hunt master, who rides at the front. I had instantly agreed to the suggestion, while at the same time wondering what on earth I was letting us in for.

I was working away in Newcastle at the time, covering the Sharon Beshenivsky police officer murder trial. When I got back home on the Friday night, the first thing I did was go to see Daniel. He looked the picture of health. His dark coat gleamed and his big white blaze shone. But there was something different about him. In my absence, Jenny had arranged for him to be hogged, that is to have his mane shaved off. Etiquette dictates that horses have to have their manes plaited for hunting. Daniel's bog-brush mane was impossible to plait and he would never have co-operated anyway, so it had to go. The thick feather had been removed from his legs and he had been given a smart hunter clip. I had never seen him without his mane and I was surprised by how much his new appearance suited him. He looked fantastic. Ruth McLaughlin, who was now managing the livery yard and was responsible for Daniel's new look, described it as 'slinky and snake-like'.

The morning of the meet was clear and fine, ideal hunting conditions. I wore a white shirt, with three T-shirts underneath to keep out the cold, a black tie and an old tweed jacket. The pair of us may have looked the part, but I didn't feel it. Jenny asked if I was nervous.

'I think the word is scared,' I replied. Shit scared, actually.

Esme offered some good advice: 'Keep your wits about you, don't get in anyone's way and don't forget your manners.'

Minutes later, I ill-manneredly got in the way of The Black Mare when an overexcited Daniel rudely tried to barge past as we made our way, with ten other horses from our yard, down the hill to the village.

It's odd how horses get so excited about hunting and seem to sense when they are going to take part. The Black Mare still prances and snorts when she hears a distant blast from the horn. She once grew about six feet when a man's mobile phone sounded and the ring tone was a hunting horn.

That morning, Daniel knew something special was about to take place. He couldn't have known what it was but the other horses did and he fed on their excitement. For riders, hunting is the chance to gallop without restraint across the countryside, and to leap whatever is in your way, if you are brave or daft enough. Similarly, the horses love the opportunity to let go and do what is natural to them. Daniel was no exception. As we jogged down the hill, he was almost pulling my arms out of their sockets. It was a side of Daniel I had never experienced before. The prophecy that hunting would bring out the best in him was already bearing fruit.

The meet was in the car park at a pub in the village. Ninety horses and riders would be gathering there. I was told it would be a cavalry charge when they set off. I had been reading a book on the Crimean War and the Charge of the Light Brigade came readily to mind. The thought did nothing for my jangling nerves.

The car park was a seething mass of horse and mankind. Daniel became hemmed in on all sides. Some young horses would have panicked and maybe kicked out. But he took it all in his stride, standing calmly and soaking up the atmosphere. His high opinion of himself came to the fore. This was just the sort of grand occasion that befitted his importance. Or so he reckoned.

I was less sure of myself. When the pre-cavalry charge trays of drinks and nibbles came round, I declined the sausages and fruit cake but gulped down two generous measures of port. They may have had something to do with the cool pose I struck for the photographer. But inside I felt like Edvard Munch's agonised image in *The Scream*.

The master of the hunt climbed the steps to a wooden-railed balcony to deliver his welcoming speech. It was jolly nice but the throng of riders just wanted to let their horses go. Me included.

Then a path was cleared and the baying hounds came purposefully through. The moment of truth was almost upon us. The horn blared its echoing and repeated call to arms. Horses reared up with their equally tense riders, both poised to spring forward, and a ripple of anticipation surged audibly through the watching crowd.

All of a sudden, the whole car park was moving as riders fought for position. I had been told there was less chance of being caught up in the mayhem if I got near the front. But we found ourselves inching our way out of the car park from the back.

From among the eager spectators, a couple wished me good luck.

'We'll need it. It's the first time for both of us. He's only four,' I told them.

Then we were out on the street and trotting in the pack. From nowhere a gap appeared and I pointed Daniel at it. He needed no second asking. In a moment we were through and picking up speed. The clatter of hooves on the tarmac, from horses all around us, echoed noisily. Daniel was up for it. We weren't just keeping up, we were overtaking others. More gaps appeared and we went through them. Before long we were halfway up the pack. Daniel was loving it, and so was I. The Black Mare loomed up alongside.

'He's going really well,' shouted Esme.

The scarlet coats and the hounds up at the front were coming into view. Little Daniel's legs were rattling along.

Then disaster struck. A few yards ahead of us, a horse lost its footing on the slippery road surface and went crashing to the ground. The rider was hurled into the road. The horse picked itself up, thankfully with nothing more serious than grazed knees. The bloodied rider lay motionless for a few moments, then painfully rose to his knees. People dashed to his aid and, as we passed, I saw it was a friend from our yard. He was in his sixties and a fortnight earlier had suffered two painful falls out hunting. The previous night he had been undecided about whether to go to the Newcomers meet but I had told him I was relying on him to look after me. Now I felt guilty. He had landed in hospital with a broken wrist and a damaged shoulder. Daniel and I had to look after ourselves.

We kept up with the frantic pace for several miles until stony country lanes slowed us down, Daniel at that time did not wear shoes. But then we reached the fields. Ahead we could see the huntsmen flying up a grassy hill on the first gallop. Then it was our turn. I let Daniel go and he charged up the hill as if going into battle. Horses were on either side of us but he was keeping pace.

At the top of the hill were three jumps. They were all big, too big for us. And anyway, we were under strict instructions from the worried ladies, no jumping allowed. Around us horses were jumping, others were refusing, some were spinning in a frantic frenzy and a number of riders parted company with their mounts. It was mayhem and Daniel added to it, hurtling down the hill in the direction of the biggest jump. I heard David Horton shouting: 'Watch out, Steve,' as we bore down on a flock of sheep.

I managed to pull Daniel up and we stood there, both of us wondering what to do next. I was thinking about whether I should defy our orders and go for the jump. Three horses approached the fence. All refused it. My mind was made up.

'Not today, Dan,' I said, as we trotted through the gate.

The Black Mare forged through the chaos to leap cleanly and enthusiastically over the jump. Very often it was she who galloped ahead to give less committed horses a bold and fluent lead over daunting obstacles. It is in her blood and she was never more in her element than when out hunting.

It was an exhilarating experience for Daniel and I and there were many more during our season of hunting. We joined the hunt on four occasions and I have strong memories of them all.

There was the first hell-for-leather gallop up the hill at the start of one meet. I followed close behind Esme on The Black Mare and, as we burst through the first gate, they raced off to the left side of a thin line of trees. Daniel pelted up the other side. It set the tone for a hunt with plenty of galloping.

Another time, we were hurtling (for Daniel) across a field when we both realised in alarm that we had charged on to a short plateau with a drop off the end. I just had time to clamp my legs round Daniel's sides and sit tight as he leapt off and, not even breaking stride, galloped on. It was terrifying and magnificent. I also remember standing around waiting in any number of fields, getting colder and colder as the biting wind blew through every layer of clothing.

Overall, it was a marvellous experience, but not one I would like to repeat on Alexander. He must have hunted in order to qualify to run in point-to-point races, and it would suit a horse of his athleticism and breeding. But the thought of him galloping enthusiastically at those big fences is daunting and I couldn't take the risk of us having a nasty accident. But it had been another step in my quest to become a better rider and it did Daniel the world of good, giving him confidence and improving his fitness. We were ready for the next stage – the biggest one in the area.

8

Trials And Tribulations

Coniston! The name is synonymous with Cheltenham or Badminton to equestrians in our locality. Coniston Hunter Trials, held in early October each year, is the event everyone wants to do well at. Like National Hunt racing's Cheltenham Festival, and the four days at Badminton for professional eventers, it is the goal many local riders target at the start of the season. It is a place where dreams can come true or be shattered in the blink of an eye of a very public gaze.

The Bannister family opens up the picturesque grounds at Coniston Hall, near Skipton, for scores of equestrians to tackle the cross-country fences as they gallop around the edge of the lake, with enthusiastic crowds watching on. Anyone who is anyone in the area turns up for the grand occasion. The equestrian eyes of the district are upon you as you take on the course, David Horton's tongue-in-cheek descriptions of each step of your journey booming out from the commentary box, positioned opposite the demanding second-fence ski jump. Going round the Coniston course can be a few minutes' rollercoaster ride of terror and elation. It is not a place to fail but a magical place to have success. Our family has tasted both triumph and disaster there.

When Jenny arrived in the area, Coniston was a mystery to her. The first time she heard about it was soon after coming to the livery yard when The Black Mare had ringworm. Pat Fitton expressed her concerns that other horses would have to be quarantined and miss Coniston Hunter Trials. Jenny had no idea what it was, or why it was so important. But with Pat riding two horses at the event, she soon became aware of the great excitement surrounding the occasion.

On the day, Pat ended up in the slimy water of the ditch beneath the big trakehner fence. Dripping wet, but completely unfazed, she offered some sound advice: 'You have to have full commitment, even if the 'oss doesn't!'

The following year, Keith Rosier, a seasoned Coniston competitor, rode the inexperienced Black Mare round the Pre-Novice course, completing with just two stops. When it comes to riding, Keith is my talisman. While Ruby Walsh is my favourite professional jockey, Keith, who rode in point-to-point races, is my local hero. He was one of those I particularly watched in the school when I was trying to pick up riding tips. His was the style I most hoped to emulate, sitting quietly with soft hands and not interfering with a horse when it jumped. Even now, when we study new photos of me jumping, the greatest compliment Jenny can pay me is: 'You look like Keith.'

He has always given me great encouragement with my riding and it was Keith I teamed up with for my proudest day at Coniston, in 2008. That year was a remarkable one for him. There were so many entries for the Pre-Novice class – well over 100 riders – it was divided into two sections. Keith won them both, on his own horse, Black Jack, and on The Black Mare.

Keith is cool under pressure and a masterful tactician. An engineer by profession, he has a mathematical brain and manages to calculate how to get the optimum time by working out where to make the wider turns and ease the horse back if it is a quick galloper, or where to cut corners and kick on if it is a bit slower.

I always argue that Keith saved his best until last in 2008 when he and Nicola's handsome bay horse Salmon Loch (Sam) teamed up with Daniel and I for the Pairs.

It was Keith who suggested I had a go and volunteered to partner me. It was a generous gesture, given that he would likely have made it a hat-trick of wins on the day with a different Pairs partner.

We managed a practice session a couple of weeks before, but I was not convinced all would go well at Coniston. Nevertheless, I didn't share Jenny's utter pessimism. She feared Daniel and I would be a disastrous combination there. I had hope, which was based on the horse's character.

Local event rider and equestrian teacher David Elms, who regularly helped Daniel and his riders, called him 'lazy and arrogant'. It was a fair description. But within that arrogance lay my hope. I believed there was a good chance he would soak up the atmosphere and importance of the event and decide it was the big stage he deserved, and therefore perform. I hoped he would take an 'of course I can do that' attitude into the big fences. He would either love it or loathe it. There would be no in-between.

I hated most of the day. Because the Pairs is the last class, it would be late in the afternoon before we got our turn. We went along in the morning to watch Keith and others go round. But the long wait was terrible. Coniston, on Daniel, was by far the biggest challenge I had faced. The fences are big, solid and unforgiving, and the pressure is intense. I felt physically sick, could not eat, could barely watch and could not get back to the yard quickly enough to prepare Daniel for the short trip to get him there.

Loading Daniel was a nightmare. He stubbornly refused to go in the trailer. I thought my day had ended before it had begun. It took seven people to finally shove him in. In the process, he stood on the end of my riding boot leaving an imprint that is still there today.

At the time it was not encouraging for the task that lay ahead. But with hindsight it was actually a good sign. Over the years, I came to realise that when Daniel walked amicably into the trailer he usually switched off at the event. When he kicked up a fuss at loading, he tended to be up for it when we got there. And so it proved.

When Jenny had towed the trailer on to the showground and we opened the side panel, Daniel's head appeared and his neck craned to watch a competitor jumping the third fence. His ears twitched at the sound of the commentary. He was definitely interested.

I had spent most of the day shaking with nerves. But when I got on Daniel, I suddenly felt calm. I could now get on with my fate, the waiting was over. But more than that, I could feel I had a horse beneath me, a horse that was keen and raring to go, a horse who felt that this was a place deserving of him. The arrogant bugger loved it!

He was keen as mustard as we trotted round the collecting ring and hopped over the practice fence, with Keith and Sam. We walked down the grassy hill and began to circle at the start, waiting for the signal to go. Sam was calm, but every time we circled to face the front, Daniel wanted to drag us on our way. He could barely contain himself.

Finally, we were called in to line up together and the starter counted us down.

'Three-Two-One – Good luck!'

I eased the reins and Daniel shot forward enthusiastically, alongside Sam. We had 18 obstacles to negotiate, including the ski jump, a spruce hurdle with a ditch in front of it, a wall and The Pen where you jump in over one fence and out over another. A successful Pairs combination will jump the fences side by side where possible. We sailed over the first fence together. It was the only one we would jump as a team.

Halfway towards the second fence, the rather daunting ski jump, Daniel began to back off and we fell behind Sam and Keith.

'Keep your leg on and keep him moving forward,' Keith shouted back.

The nearer we got to the fence, the less Daniel liked it. It was a major crisis and a dramatic early test of my riding skills. I began booting Dan furiously, then gave him one hard crack behind my leg with the whip, and twice shouted: 'Get on!' It was not the place to have a stop, right in front of the commentary box, the massed crowds, the refreshment tent, Nicola, David Horton, the Bannisters, and all.

With two strides to the fence, I sat back and shoved. It was now or never. And suddenly Daniel was leaping. A photograph taken by *Craven Herald* reporter Lesley Tate, on her digital camera from the other side of the fence, shows us coming in to land. I am still shoving. Daniel is desperately stretching out his front legs to greet the ground, his top notch of hair standing on end and a look of terror in his eyes.

It was the turning point. Daniel clearly felt that if he could jump that, he could jump anything. He happily went round, following in Sam's wake and leaping anything in front of him. After negotiating The Pen in fine style, I gave him two big pats on the neck as we cantered down towards the lake, making a reality of something I had dreamed of doing.

With three fences to go we cantered past the front of the Hall and Daniel began to lag further behind Sam.

'Give the lazy bugger a crack!' Keith called out.

I did and Daniel responded with one last effort, picking up pace as he realised we were nearly at the finish. We flew over the final log, as it turned out a fence from the big Open class. An official photo of the last jump shows Dan with his front legs tucked up under his chest, his hair flying, his white socks brown from the mud and white sweat on his neck and shoulder (a first, and subsequently rare occurrence!).

'This is the best day of my life,' I said as we received our sixth-place rosette. It will always remain one of my finest riding achievements.

Jenny told me years later that she hid in a Portaloo before the start of my round because she could not bear to witness what she was certain would be disaster and humiliation.

Daniel and I went back to Coniston in 2009 with new Pairs partners. This time there was no rosette, but I was delighted to go clear for a second year running and, unlike the previous year, I had not taken any of the easier alternative fences.

Getting Daniel round Coniston was testament to the improvement in my riding. But I knew he did not have the speed or enthusiasm to challenge for cross-country prizes. With my ambitions raised, I needed to find a horse that would.

9

Bringing Up Baby

While Daniel had made steady, if unremarkable, progress as a showjumper and possible cross-country horse, bringing up his younger brother, Baby Horse, had proved more complex.

Baby is an unusual and striking-looking horse; a rusty reddish colour with a rocking horse mane and hazel eyes that seem to develop a mad, amber look. He has a big white star and stockings on both beefy back legs.

When the young brothers arrived at the livery yard, David Horton sized them up with his measuring stick and found Daniel to be 14.3 hands, while Baby was 14.1 hands. But Baby just kept on growing. Probably part-carthorse, he turned into a strapping 16-hand chunk with pit props for legs and an obdurate immovability. The name Baby became ridiculous but as it seemed to suit his character, it stuck.

Baby was incredibly stubborn and frustrating. Trying to move him when he was not inclined to was like trying to shift half a house. All the shoving and pushing in the world would barely budge him. And, inhabiting his own dream-like world, he had precious little spacial awareness, invariably plonking his great dinnerplate hooves on your feet and agonisingly leaving them there, not because he was malicious but simply because he had not noticed.

But Baby's unique persona and air of baffled vulnerability meant you somehow felt compelled to go that extra mile for him. I have scars on my forearm after putting myself between a barbed wire fence and an unnerved Baby when a speeding van bore down on us as we walked him on long-reins. My daughter, Emma, always had a soft spot for him. Though she, and my son Ben, do not ride, they are confident and capable around the horses. Emma made a particular pet of Baby, sparing time to groom him, and helping to nurse him through a life-threatening infection.

Our plans for Baby were often hit by setbacks. He seemed to attract unusual difficulties. If there was something nasty to get, he would get it, like grass mites. The little blighters plagued the big chap in the summer months. At first we thought the furious stamping of his back legs in the stable, and the scrubbing of the backs of them against the water tank in the field, were part of his eccentric behaviour. We had never even heard of grass mites and so had no idea what signs to look out for. We found the best solution was sulphur and pig oil, mixed to the texture of soft margarine, which we would liberally smear on his legs, turning them a bright shade of yellow. He looked like he was wearing football socks as he walked off to the field, dripping yellow goo behind him.

Another of Baby's problems demanded a more unusual solution. He went through a period of extreme head flinging that culminated with him breaking his nose when he hit the stone lintel above his stable door. Even when we had the lintel raised he still managed to somehow reach it. Our answer was to fit a hinged metal grille across the space between his door and the lintel. It was a shame to pen him in but his safety had to come first.

The metal grille became bowed like a dinosaur's ribcage when Baby began to vigorously rub and scratch his big backside on it. One morning, we found his nocturnal shoving had wedged the metal against the stone surround, leaving him entombed in his box. The grille resembled the battered underwater cage in the *Jaws* film after the big fish had attacked it. I managed to free him by borrowing a large hammer and delivering a hefty swipe.

His habit of violently throwing his head in the air made loading him into the trailer, already an ordeal through his stubbornness, a near impossibility. If we had any competitive plans for him, however modest, they usually went out of the window because we simply could not get him there.

After a while, Baby settled down and the head flinging stopped as suddenly as it had started. We were unable to trust him not to injure himself straight away, so Jenny fashioned an eye-catching 'Easter bonnet' to protect him. It was made from a headcollar with a leather poll guard and a noseband swathed in Vet Wrap, the layers of padding secured with silver duct tape. Baby looked like an outlandish monster from *Dr Who* but he was happy enough to wear it.

Despite his eccentricities I had high hopes that the strapping Baby could be my cross-country horse of the future. I even dreamed that one day I might win Coniston Hunter Trials on him.

There were glimpses of greatness that gave my ambitions some credence. Baby enjoyed his trips to Craven Country Ride, paddling happily in the water, leaping off the multi-bank and jumping the fences with enthusiasm, so much so that I have the dubious distinction of being the first, and only, rider to be jumped off him. I put him at an inviting brush fence but was unimpressed by the way he blundered through it nose-first, scattering fronds of conifer. We approached it again and I asked him for more effort. He provided it, bounding in and taking a giant leap that unseated me and propelled my whip skywards like a bonfire night rocket. Apart from a bitten tongue and a couple of bruises, I was unscathed. Unlike his brother, who always charged off, reins and stirrups flapping, after unseating his rider, Baby simply began to graze.

Previously, I had a ridiculous accident in the cross-country field when he put his head down and shook himself vigorously, causing me to slide headfirst between his ears, taking the bridle with me. Baby did not bat an eyelid.

Another daft incident occurred when I tackled a new fence, a solid rail between the cross-country field and the showjumps field. Baby poddled in and heaved his front legs over the two-foot-wide fence. But his back legs failed to follow and we found ourselves straddling the fence with our front end in the showjumps field and our back end in the cross-country field. Baby blinked in momentary surprise, then bent his head to graze. After several minutes, I persuaded him to lift his front legs, while reversing from behind, and we got free.

'At least you've taught its front legs to jump,' commented one chum.

Baby's modest collection of four rosettes, one for completing the Christmas Trail at Craven Country Ride and the rest hard-won after stumbling and scrambling attempts at an 18-inch course in our livery yard's Clear Round competition, belied the cross-country potential I yearned to see fulfilled.

Baby was strong and enthusiastic, and he could jump. He had tantalised me by cantering over a 2ft 3in Clear Round course at Gargrave Show, his first public appearance, and by enthusiastically hurdling a daunting 'window box' fence of Busy Lizzies at Craven Country Ride. But would he step up and be the competition horse I needed? My riding had improved, and my confidence with it.

Now I needed to test the fledgling partnership.

10

Somerford Park

I had heard a lot about Somerford Park before I ever went there. The prestigious equestrian centre in Cheshire hosts major eventing and dressage competitions, as well as regular horse camps where you are taught to showjump and cross-country jump by professional riders. It has an almost mythical reputation with ordinary riders like me. The reality did not disappoint.

Somerford camps are a learning curve, a real challenge to horse and jockey and you are pushed hard by the instructors. But there is plenty of fun along the way. My first visit to Somerford was in 2007. I took Daniel, and it was another success for us. Passing through the impressive entrance gates to Somerford Park for the first time was like entering some mystical land. It was as if I had gone through the wardrobe into a C. S. Lewis kind of equestrian fantasy world. As we trundled along the wide, sweeping driveway there seemed to be large outdoor schools everywhere I looked. And, disappearing into the distance beyond the vista of perfect green paddocks, could be glimpsed the huge and varied obstacles of the cross-country course.

Following the signs, we passed the sizeable equestrian shop, an Aladdin's Cave for the ladies, and drove into the main yard area, a hive of activity, with horses, wagons, riders and staff at every turn. In front of us, we sighted yet more schools but our route was to the left, past the wooden clubhouse and a stable block, and into the adjoining field where we parked up.

On the first afternoon you enjoy the Farm Ride. This is the fun bit where you get to ride around the beautiful country estate, hacking through woods, crossing streams, clattering across footbridges, enjoying long grassland canters and jumping rustic fences of all shapes and sizes, if you want to.

Daniel was completely unfazed by the new experience. As usual, he appreciated that it was an important place and decided to make the most of it. He seemed in his element round the Farm Ride and was happy to jump some decent-sized logs. Nor did he object to his bed of shavings, having always slept on straw at home. He hungrily munched his supper and, when I slipped out from the clubhouse later that evening to make sure he was all right, I found him happily settled and relaxed in his new surroundings.

The next day was a triumph and the pack of photographs I keep very safely show how the little chap excelled on the cross-country course. It is an amazing fact that I was the only one in our group who did not fall off during the camp. The good money would certainly have been on me to be the first to tumble. Instead, there is an unlikely photo of Daniel enthusiastically launching himself, ears pricked, out of the water complex from two strides out, while in the background two young lady riders, who had come to grief, stand holding their horses.

A further sequence of images illustrates Daniel's unique jump-jet method of leaping. The first shows him anxiously clearing a wooden rail by more than double its two-foot height, his front legs tucked up under his chest; the next sees him plummeting like a stone, his forward momentum sharply declining; and the final shot has his front legs, straight as a ruler, seeking the ground just the other side of the log fence while he flicks his back legs high above it. Throughout the sequence, I look less than stylish, arms akimbo in my shabby green and blue wet-through anorak. But my seat and leg look surprisingly secure and my expression is oddly serene.

Generally more at home when showjumping, Daniel performed wonderfully in that phase during the two days and I returned home, clutching my prized photos and with lots of excited tales to tell.

The following year, Daniel and I had the same instructor, Chris Ward, who seemed to have a soft spot for the horse. Things went well enough but I came away a bit disappointed. After the success of our first visit, I had wanted to push on further. But, though there were no disasters, it didn't really happen for us and we found ourselves in an unsuitable group with people out of our class who weren't inclined to give us much backing. Probably, the reality was that Daniel and I had gone as far as we were going to.

In 2009, I switched horses for Somerford and took Baby, with genuine hope that he would prove himself to be the cross-country partner I so much wanted him to be. Preparations for his Somerford Park debut went well. His varied training programme included blundering round a tiny course at the yard's Clear Round showjumping competition; a demanding schooling session with local eventer David Elms; and calling at local hostelries during long, fitness-building hacks out.

Jenny bought a new saddle, a brown leather working-hunter classic, to encourage Baby to put his back into his cross-country work. At one point, he was being exercised twice a day and there were encouraging trips to Craven Country Ride, where he jumped a roll top, leapt a solid barrel fence that was part of the previous year's Coniston Hunter Trials course, and even tackled a 'skinny' barrel, although the hefty chap managed to snap the marker flag clean off.

Baby had a unique cross-country jumping style. When he saw a fence, his mad, amber eyes lit up. He galumphed eagerly at it, head on the floor, then launched himself over and stopped dead on the other side. He looked round for the next one, gathered himself and trundled off again. His technique might be unusual but it seemed to be working.

His final training exercise was a trip to the cross-country course at Broomhill, near Clitheroe, where he happily jumped round before bizarrely spinning and bolting off during a rider change. The unedifying spectacle of Baby lumbering about on his own prompted an exasperated Esme to remark: 'There's always a boy on the loose.'

Nothing was ever straightforward with Baby, but within his parallel universe the training programme was relatively routine and there seemed no reason not to be optimistic about Somerford.

There was particular excitement about this horse camp. Not only was Baby making his debut, but my daughter Sophie was going for the first time. She was taking Daniel. A keen and natural rider,

Sophie was excited by the challenge. The Black Mare, a seasoned Somerford veteran, was also making the trip, so there was quite a family party in prospect.

The motorway journey to the camp was tough for a nervous Jenny, with driving rain, blustery wind, the constant thunder of passing juggernauts, and two precious horses in the trailer. But she gritted her teeth and delivered us safely, some two hours later, through the imposing iron gates of Somerford Park Farm.

It was then that things began to go wrong. After trundling into the main yard, Jenny switched off the engine of our old red Land Rover Defender while we sought advice about where to park. When she tried to start up again there was nothing but a click from the ignition. The Land Rover stubbornly refused to show any hint of life.

We dejectedly off-loaded Baby and Daniel and led them away while the vehicle was ignominiously bump-started to enable us to park up in the camping field. The next day, we summoned the AA who fixed the Land Rover ready for the return journey.

Things went from bad to worse when it came to our riding lessons. Baby and I were in the same group as Sophie and Daniel, in the novice class. Our teacher was international event rider Rachel Bayliss, a former European gold medallist.

We began with the showjumping, never something Baby had really got his head round. It proved disastrous. While Daniel did everything that was asked of him, Baby refused to move. It was all I could do to shove him towards a jump. The effort to get him over, or usually through it, and then boot him towards the next obstacle left me exhausted after only ten minutes. The longer the lesson went on the more sullen and stubborn Baby became. It looked like being a very long two days.

After a reviving lie-down and energy-giving bananas for lunch, I was ready for the afternoon session. I felt all hope was not lost. Baby had never seen the point of showjumping but he had been enjoying his cross-country and that seemed to be where our future lay. I felt sure this would be his strong suit and at least we would get some good photos out of it.

To my surprise, and bitter disappointment, Baby was no better in the afternoon than he had been in the morning. I could hardly get a trot out of him and he had no enthusiasm for jumping the fences. He had completely switched off. He had decided that Somerford wasn't for him and he simply was not going to play ball.

That evening, Sophie was able to enjoy a collection of wonderful photos from her first Somerford visit, showing she and Daniel leaping in and out of the water over a roll top and hurdling a red-roofed house. All I had to show for my determined efforts was four shots of us plodding through the water and a rather fetching snap of Baby stepping over a little bank out of the sunken road. Even in that one, his mad, amber eyes seemed to blaze with resentment.

The next day I tried wearing spurs for the showjumping. Spurs are not something I like to use and I have very rarely worn them but someone suggested them as a possible way to get Baby to move forward. Sadly, all they achieved was to mark his flanks, making me feel guilty about the whole event. I didn't use them again.

So that was it. The great adventure had turned into a total disaster. My hopes were in tatters, along with my cross-country dream. My despair was complete when it was time to leave. Everything was packed. All that remained was to load Baby. We thought he wouldn't be so bad, as he was going home and he had clearly hated Somerford.

Not so. Baby planted himself in front of the trailer ramp and refused to move. Nothing the five of us tried to do could budge him. Almost in tears, we begged for help and eventually managed to shovel him inside. It was the final straw. Much as we all loved him, Baby just did not seem fit for purpose. If he wouldn't move or load, how were we ever going to compete on him? As Rachel Bayliss put it: 'If you stop pedalling, it doesn't go!'

I left the camp with the words of my instructor ringing in my ears: 'He needs another job and you need another horse!' The next time I went to Somerford, I took Alexander.

11

Mother And Son

On a cold winter's afternoon, at a humble racecourse in Shropshire, a feisty chestnut mare was cantered down to the start for a three-mile steeplechase. The eight-year-old racehorse, Gun Shot, was normally a hurdler and she had won three times over the smaller obstacles. She had also finished second on two occasions and had a third place from her 16 hurdle races.

This time she was to tackle the big fences. Her only previous steeplechase had seen her finish tenth of 11 runners, a huge 86 lengths behind the winner. But that was early in her career and her trainer, Norman Babbage, felt it was worth another go. The bookies had her down as an 11-1 outsider in the betting. Her regular jockey, Jodie Mogford, was in the saddle. He had ridden her six times before, twice to victory.

But the Annual Members Chase (Showcase Handicap), run at Ludlow at 2.10 on January 3, 2003, a Class E race worth less than £7,000 to the winner, was to be the last that Gun Shot would run. Just over a year later, she gave birth to the first of three foals, a big chestnut colt who would become known as Alexander and be the horse of my dreams.

As the race began, Jodie Mogford held up Gun Shot at the back, looking to give her the chance to settle down. But she began to get behind and jumping mistakes at the fourth and fifth fences did not help her cause. The tough, tenacious mare battled on and began to make headway again, but she weakened towards the end of the race and trailed in last of the nine finishers. Norman Babbage was quick to recognise it was time to give Gun Shot the chance of another life, this time as a mother.

Gun Shot had run a total of 19 times under racing rules, over three years, and earned £15,735. Her highest official rating had been 101. It had been a modest but worthy career. Mr Babbage, who trained in Gloucestershire, said: 'She was a good hurdler, but she was no good at the fences. She just didn't handle them in that last race. And by then, she'd had enough of racing.'

I had always suspected that Alexander's occasional mad moments bore the influence of his mother, a theory confirmed by Norman Babbage. 'Gun Shot's mother, Real Beauty, had five foals, all mares, and all psychopathic.'

He recalled when he first saw the mare: 'We went to buy sheep from a friend. Gun Shot and her sister, O My Love, who had been trained by Henrietta Knight, were in a field there and we bought them.

'Gun Shot was strong-willed, determined and genuine on the racecourse. When she was in the mood she wouldn't be beaten, not because of her ability but because she wouldn't give up,' said Mr Babbage.

Gun Shot was sired by Gunner B, a successful Flat horse in the 1970s who won nearly half of his 33 races, including the Group 1 Eclipse Stakes at Sandown under the training of Henry Cecil. Gunner B was equally successful in his long career at stud, siring a host of winners including Champion Hurdler Royal Gait and Grand National winner Red Marauder – Alexander's 'uncles' – and becoming the oldest active thoroughbred sire in Europe at the ripe old age of 29.

Gun Shot had a wild streak in her. According to Norman Babbage, she was named by the man who broke her in, who said she was 'so dangerous she ought to be shot.' Mr Babbage remembered one day at the races when he spotted a rogue straw in her tail as she was being walked round the pre-race parade ring.

'In front of the saddle she was fine, but she didn't like you touching her behind the saddle. She could be lethal, kicking out at you. I tried to pick my moment to get rid of the straw with a dandy brush, but she kicked out, mashing my hand and launching the dandy brush 150 metres through the air, out of the parade ring and into the racecourse stable yard!'

But she also had her quieter moments. 'She was a character and when she was in season she would be dopey and would rest her head on your back,' he recalled, fondly. 'She had ability and won for me three times. She had the heart of a lion but she needed small courses to perform. I never took her to a big course. She was a lovely mare. I thought the world of her.'

After retiring her, Mr Babbage sold Gun Shot as a broodmare to the Cookson family of horse breeders and farmers in Kendal, Cumbria. She had the run of a big field at the back of their farm.

James Cookson said: 'We were looking for a brood mare and she was advertised in the *Racing Post*. We rang Norman Babbage. He sent her up. We liked her and bought her.

'She was a bit fiery, a bit of a sod. If feeding time was four o'clock, it had to be four o'clock, not five to or five past. If it wasn't on time she would kick off. But she was a one-man horse and if I went to feed her she was fine.

'We sent her to the sire Alflora, at the Shade Oak Stud in Shropshire. We had put a couple of mares to him before and liked him.'

Alflora had been successful as a Flat horse, winning five races, earning more than a quarter of a million pounds, and finishing sixth in the 1992 Derby, won by Dr Devious. His career at stud has been even more prolific and he has been Britain's leading sire of steeplechasers five times.

On March 23, 2004, Alexander was born at the Cooksons' farm. He was christened Alfie, after his father.

'He was quite a dark chestnut when he was a foal. He was an absolute little star. He was really soft, you could do anything with him. He was halter broken at a week old and he was fine,' said Mr Cookson.

'You could shout "Alfie" across the field and he would come running with his mum. Because he was the first foal he had a fair bit of time spent on him and he was as soft and gentle as anything could be.'

At seven months old, Alfie went to the horse sales at Tattersalls in Ireland but was not sold, and he returned to the Cookson farm.

Gun Shot had a second foal, a younger brother for Alexander, called Morecambe Bay, who has been a novice hurdler and chaser and is now point-to-pointing. Gun Shot sadly died, aged only 11, after foaling for the third time, a filly who was fostered at the Cookson farm.

Alexander, or Alfie, lived a peaceful life in the field until he was three years old when he went to Carlisle to be broken in by trainer and former professional jump jockey, Brian Storey. Brian was the first person to ride him and he was pleased with the canters they had on the gallop track at his yard.

'He'd had nothing done with him and he was a big backward horse,' he said. 'I had him for three months and got him going. He was a lovely horse to break in. He had a lovely temperament, very laid-back. But he was a typical backward young horse who needed time.

'He was a lovely, lovely horse. He used to jump the pools and puddles. He had really good breeding. He looked the part. We thought he just wanted time. He could have been anything, the way he was bred. He was just very laid-back, a really nice horse. I thought he wouldn't come to his best until he was seven or eight years old.'

Alfie returned to the Cooksons and was turned out in the field. Mr Cookson said: 'He was a bit immature. He needed to fill out a bit. We just left him. We didn't do anything with him, we were letting him grow. The intention was to sell him.'

In August 2008, aged four, Alfie went to the Doncaster Bloodstock Sales but was withdrawn from sale. Soon afterwards, between his fourth and fifth birthdays, he was sold to Ian and Karen Conroy, who own a small stud farm overlooking the estuary at Grange-over-Sands in Cumbria.

Ian and Karen have become important and trusted friends and were indirectly responsible for leading Alexander into my life. Indeed, without their kindness and patience his life could have taken an altogether different path and I might never have fulfilled my dream.

Alfie had been recommended to them by local racehorse trainer Jimmy Moffatt, who had seen him at the Cookson farm and liked the look of him. Although he had been backed by Brian Storey, he had then been left to grow and develop and was still a big, backward horse living in a cow barn.

'He was just a fat chestnut horse with a big belly,' Ian recalled, a description that is hard to visualise now.

Alfie also had an attitude problem that led to him being rechristened.

'We nicknamed him Herman Monster because he was a bit gormless,' said Ian. 'He didn't want to do anything and wouldn't even leave the yard at first. He would rear and go into reverse. He went backward faster than he went forward. He would even sit down while you were on him.

'Herman seemed to suit him as a name because at that stage he was just big and rather stupid. But he was very cunning when he didn't want to do something. He would reverse towards a parked car – that told me he knew what he was doing.'

The reversing at speed was something I too would experience. It was an odd, but calculated, tactic and seemed to indicate his fragile nature, as well as a stubborn streak that no doubt came from his mother.

But Ian and Karen persevered and managed to persuade him to leave the confines of the yard. Karen recalled: 'I kept riding him to the gate and then turning him away from it. He was obviously very puzzled. He began thinking, "Why don't we just go through it?" I had no trouble with him after that.'

'Herman' enjoyed his rides down the country roads with Karen and seemed happy with his new routine. His fitness and weight improved and he began to look more like a racehorse.

Ian and Karen breed horses for the racing world and they had been contacted by somebody who wanted to own a racehorse. 'Herman' was a prime candidate. Trainer Martin Todhunter, who runs a professional jumps yard in Cumbria, came to look at him. He liked what he saw, was impressed with his breeding, and took him on. But his stay there was brief. His attitude problem resurfaced and he took a dislike to the horse walker, refusing to move and bringing it to a halt. Raceyard staff, fearing the horse would cause the motor to burn out, were forced to chase him round and get him off it. It was clear, at just five years old, he was still backward, both physically and mentally, and needed more time.

Alexander was moved on to a point-to-point yard in Durham to be trained for amateur steeplechasing the following year, when he would be six. He must have been hunted that winter to qualify to race.

He made his racing debut, under the name Adelphi Warrior, in a 3m Open Maiden race, for horses that haven't won, on February 7, 2010, at Witton Castle in Durham. There were seven runners and Alexander was a 5-1 chance in the betting. He trailed in last of the six finishers, a considerable distance behind the winner. His jockey reported he had jumped well but he hadn't been quick enough between his fences. That day, a fast-finishing horse called Hunt

Ball – who would later win national acclaim – was just pipped into second place.

Hunt Ball would start as 2-1 favourite in Alexander's second, and final, race at Dalston, Cumbria, on Saturday, March 6, 2010, also an Open Maiden race. There were 15 runners and Alexander was well fancied at 4-1 in the betting. The going was described as good, softish in places in the straight and becoming sticky. I have found that Alexander goes better on firmer ground. He is a big horse and struggles a bit when it is soft and heavy. That must have been the case at Dalston. Though he jumped well again, he got behind and his jockey pulled him up.

And that was the end of his brief and unspectacular racing career. The owner returned him to Ian and Karen. They sold him to a friend who had taken a shine to him.

Within weeks, he was with me.

12

Bye Bye Baby

Following the disastrous trip to Somerford, the whole family agonised over Baby Horse's future. Above all, we had to consider his happiness. If he was totally unsuited to the world of competing, would it not be kinder to let him go somewhere where he could lead a quieter life? And so the painful decision was made to part with him.

It took less than a week for us to change our minds. Back home, the image of Baby stumbling reluctantly over the tiniest crossbar at Somerford faded quickly. Jenny looked at his treasured row of four rosettes and the striking photographs of him paddling in the Somerford Park water complex and decided she could not bear to let him go. We had owned him for five years and we all felt he was an essential part of the family.

Anyway, how could we explain to Daniel that he would have to be separated from the younger brother he was devoted to? The pair's affection for each other was evident when we turned Baby out in the field. With no other horse in sight, he neighed, hoping for a friendly reply. From above the tree line came a noisy response and Daniel charged down the hill, his shoes skidding and the silvery skirts of his fly rug flapping. He and Baby greeted each other affectionately before wandering off contentedly together.

Back on home ground, Baby seemed happier and more eager to impress. He consented to hours of pole and grid work in the outdoor school and long hacks and canter work to boost his fitness. He even clomped straight into the trailer for a trip to Craven Country Ride, where he jumped many of the fences left up from the Novice class at a recent hunter trial. He earned another rosette for taking part in Craven's Christmas Trail Ride, where he enthusiastically cantered up hill and down dale with his brother and clambered over a series of small logs.

Baby's new found vigour, after we added vegetable oil to his evening meals, resulted in a couple of unexpected falls from him. First, Jenny hit the deck on the lane when Baby shied violently at a group of picnicking ramblers hidden away against a dry stone wall. The hikers, who had concealed themselves to ensure their Primus stove was sheltered sufficiently to boil up a warming cup of tea on a chilly and breezy morning, were sympathetic and helpful.

'You can't trust horses at all, can you?' they said, popping up suddenly from their green and red striped camping stools to warily assist.

Then, I jumped a rail in the cross-country field by myself when Baby skidded and slammed on the brakes.

As we moved into the New Year of 2010, our thoughts again turned to future plans and what was best for us and our horses. The winter months had, as always, taken their toll. Working full-time in Bradford meant that in the dark evenings we had little time, or energy, for more than mucking out, feeding and tucking in. And the challenge on our purse-strings was always great.

With Daniel doing so well, Baby was the obvious candidate for a new home but it seemed impossible that anyone would want to take on the sheer effort of caring for and riding him. Although placid and gentle, his lack of spatial awareness, the exhausting and demoralising misery of loading him, and his inability, or unwillingness, to move along at any speed, seemed insuperable obstacles. As Ruth McLaughlin had observed years earlier, Baby was 'largely static'.

The decision to part with him finally came in the spring after Jenny and I took Baby and Daniel on a long hack out. The Yorkshire Dales countryside was at its best. We rode through rolling green meadows skirting Craven Country Ride. Wild flowers covered the banks of the lanes and the sun lit up the hills sweeping away towards Skipton and beyond. But the boys refused to move fluently forward, winding one another down with every step. We could not even coax a canter from them on a tempting green track where The Black Mare always pulled and snorted to gallop to the far gate.

To Jenny, spoilt by the keenness and speed of The Black Mare, it was a soul-sapping experience. Almost in tears of frustration, she untacked Baby at his turnout field on the way home, preferring to carry the saddle and bridle herself the last few hundred yards. It seemed less of an effort.

Something had to be done. With determination, but little hope, she advertised Baby for sale on the popular Horsemart website. The daunting task of drafting and placing the advert had to be done at work because we had no computer at home. Jenny's computer skills were shaky and she had never compiled an on-line advertisement. Trying to evade the ever-watchful eye of the *Telegraph & Argus* newsdesk team, she followed the instructions and carefully crafted a realistic and totally honest few words, with photos attached, including Baby jumping a hefty log at Craven Country Ride and the prized image, for so long propped proudly up on the kitchen mantelpiece, of him scrambling up the bank at Somerford Park.

She completed the on-line paying process and watched her creation form in cyberspace to take its place at the top of the newest list of horses for sale. She expected no response whatsoever.

What happened next was one of the most important lessons we have learned and one that stood us in good stead when having to make an even more difficult and painful decision. Our country is blessed with tens of thousands of horse-mad folk who do not want to gallop at breakneck speed out hunting, leap challenging rails and ditches or tackle daunting showjumps. Many of these 'happy hackers' do not even choose to compete. They crave a docile horse to love, care for and ride out safely with their friends.

Within minutes of the advert being placed, Jenny's mobile phone was ringing. Dozens of callers throughout the country wanted to buy Baby. Some were so desperate they were close to tears when Jenny had to put them off. Wooed by photos of the handsome, strapping chap, many wanted to hunt and even event him. Others had more modest plans but they still involved a degree of fluency and willingness over small fences or in schooling sessions.

After a time, Jenny resorted to David Elms' description of Baby as 'a backward tank' to repel the most insistent. It was a bit harsh but better than a prospective buyer ending up with an unsuitable horse. It was touching how many people thanked her for her blunt honesty. But buying a horse is a significant and very exciting commitment. The last thing we wanted was to be the cause of anger and disappointment and for poor Baby to be unceremoniously dumped back after we had given up his stable at the livery yard, always assuming he could be loaded for the return journey!

In the end, we made it simple. Baby would go to a home where his new owners had no schooling arena or set of showjumps. Less than two weeks after the advert first appeared, Mark Grunnill and Alison Oliver, from Cumbria, came to see Baby. Alison rode him down the leafy lane towards the cross-country field. Slender and gentle, she said she felt safe and secure as Baby trundled contentedly along.

Alison wanted a quiet horse to ride out from their rural home on the estuary near Grange-over-Sands. Baby would just have to hack out along the sea wall, through nearby woodland and down flat country lanes. No hills. It sounded ideal for him. Mark would also have tried riding him, but he was hobbling after suffering a serious injury. He told us his horse had reared and thrown him while he was mounting it and he had woken up in hospital.

Alison instantly fell in love with Baby and the couple collected him on Sunday, May 16, 2010, for a month-long trial with a view to buy. We arranged to visit Baby at his new home a couple of days later.

Jenny gazed sadly at his empty stable.

'What sort of horse are you looking for to replace Baby?' asked Mark, before leaving.

'We're not in any hurry,' Jenny replied. 'We'll probably wait until next year and then look for something that Steve can do some cross-country on. I fancy another black Irish horse.'

Mark looked thoughtful. Then he announced that he had just what we wanted. A young 16.3 hands chestnut ex-racehorse. The one that had landed him in hospital. Jenny was horrified. She politely told him that was the last sort of horse she would ever want to own. Five days later, Baby's large loosebox was no longer empty.

13

Hello Herman

The journey to Cumbria was uneventful. Mark's directions were precise and in little more than an hour we were nearing our destination. Mark and Alison's home, reached down a winding rural lane over a picturesque wooden bridge, was everything we could have hoped for. Their detached house was bounded by lush fields, where black and white cattle munched peacefully and calves and lambs frolicked.

The house was circled by lawns, where plump free-range hens and noisy cockerels roamed freely. A friendly dog basked in the sunshine. Across the rich pastureland could be glimpsed the estuary with its cruel but wonderful tides, close to the notorious Morecambe Bay sands where a stagecoach sank without trace in the days when horse power was everything.

Mark and Alison gave us a welcome to match the warm weather and took us straight to where Baby was grazing with a pony in a paddock beside the house. If Baby was delighted to see us, he didn't show it. We entered the field and walked towards him. There may have been recognition but there wasn't an ounce of enthusiasm. He ambled over for the obligatory mint, permitted us to pat him for a couple of minutes, then wandered off with his new friend. Clearly, he was a contented horse, which was what we were expecting and hoping for. He obviously didn't need us but Mark and Alison were very keen on him. We felt certain we had found him the right home.

We meandered back to the house and took our seats at a wooden table outside, facing the paddock and the distant estuary. The sun continued to shine. The hens strutted confidently round our feet as Alison produced an array of homemade cakes. The dog joined in the hopeful scavenging for titbits.

We sipped coffee in the sun and watched Baby tucking into the grass in the paddock just beyond the garden fence. This was the life. It seemed a million miles away from our jobs in Bradford and the criminals that inhabit our every day at work. Afterwards, we both confessed to a twinge of envy at what seemed a near perfect existence.

Mark told us about his father's career in the mounted section of the Metropolitan Police and how he now had a new job as chief steward of the British Showjumping Association. Recently, he had worked at the Horse of the Year Show, where he met many top riders and saw Katie Price warming up her dressage horses.

It was a lovely, relaxing afternoon. But for Jenny there was a rather large cloud on the horizon. Nothing had so far been said, but at the far side of the paddock was something tall, in a glinting gold fly rug and matching hat, and with a long, drooping pelican-like head. It seemed quite happy to stand basking in the spring sunshine and Jenny fervently hoped it would stay where it was.

I, too, had spotted it. It was indeed tall. It was also lean, and athletic, and orange in colour. And it looked wonderful. I prayed that our hosts were not going to forget about it.

The minutes passed. But, as the afternoon drew to a close, Mark fetched a lead rope, set forth, and brought 'Herman', for that was its name, to the gate. I was transfixed. I had never seen anything quite like it close up.

Just a couple of months earlier, I had been thrilled to meet my favourite living racehorse. I persuaded our features editor to let me write an article for our company's *Yorkshire Living* magazine on steeplechaser Mister McGoldrick, who was trained locally on Bingley Moor by Sue Smith at the home she shares with her husband, former international showjumper Harvey Smith.

Getting to see Mister McGoldrick in his stable, feed him a mint and stand holding him by his headcollar, all in the name of work, was a dream come true. But, for all his bold jumping and grim determination not to be beaten, the racing veteran did not stand out to look at. Not like Herman. The nearer you got to him, the taller he seemed to get. He had big, powerful shoulders and a similar back end, but there wasn't an ounce of fat on him. He was almost skinny. His big, light brown eyes rolled uncertainly, and rather disconcertingly. But he seemed meek enough. Not the sort of chap, on the face of it, you would expect to put you in hospital.

Mark strode to the house for a saddle and bridle. He put the bridle, kindly donated by his dad from his days in the Met, on an obedient Herman. The saddle fitted cosily over a furry brown numnah, giving Herman the appearance of a drum major's horse. He was led out of the garden and made to stand just outside the gates on the edge of the lane. I was wondering how to get on this tall orange creature when a wooden stool was produced to use as a mounting block.

Jenny, who confidently expected me to die at any moment, could only stand back and watch in dismay as I sat on my first ever racehorse. My heart was in my mouth as I stood nervously on the stool. As I pushed up to swing my leg across Herman's back, I accidentally kicked the stool backwards and it toppled to the ground with a clatter. I caught my breath, expecting the horse to react in some ridiculously athletic way that would leave me in great pain. But Mark had a strong hold on him. There was a little twitch, and then nothing. Herman was standing perfectly still, with me sitting on top of him. It was an odd feeling, unreal and yet right.

'OK?' asked Mark.

'Fine,' I replied, more nonchalantly than I felt.

Mark led us into the lane. Hardly anyone lived down this pretty backwater so the chances of meeting any traffic were remote. That was a blessing.

'Are you all right to take charge?' said Mark, knowing the answer and letting the reins go.

This was it. Here I was, 51 years old, and about to take my first ride on a racehorse. We set off down the road at a brisk walk. 'Bloody hell,' I thought. Even at the walk, the difference from the horses I had ridden before was astonishing. This bounced, and sprang, and swayed. It was alive with movement. Each step it took moved me around in the saddle in a way that was disconcerting and yet exhilarating.

Herman had an incredible rhythm and quite quickly I learned to move with it and to get in time with it. And I was loving it. We turned round and walked the other way, round a corner towards a couple of secluded houses, then retraced our steps to where we had begun. We went the other way again, but now, for the first time, we trotted. I thought, perhaps, Herman would take off with me because we were going faster. But he didn't. He just trotted in that same lovely rhythm and I joined in with the music. It was magical and I could have carried on all afternoon. But it was time to go back.

Alison was smiling. 'You suit each other perfectly,' she said. I didn't know about that but it had been great fun.

I dismounted and Herman was led away to be untacked and put back in his paddock. He ambled off to graze. He had taken it all in his long stride, almost robotically. But he was a robot with great style, that was for sure.

Fearing my mind was made up, Jenny whispered: 'I don't like its head, it's long and thin.'

'All racehorse heads are like that,' I hissed back, offended.

Already, I felt a protective bond towards this wonderful, if totally alien, orange creature. We sat down to reflect over another coffee. Mark fetched Herman's passport. It showed his racing name was Adelphi Warrior. It was, undeniably, a good name. And Mark had an answer to Jenny's last, feeble protest that her heart was set on an Irish horse: Herman's dad was Irish.

I sat at the garden table almost reverently studying the fascinating booklet. Encased in a smart, racing green-coloured binder was a real Weatherbys passport with details of a real racehorse. Herman's mum was called Gun Shot. His dad was Alflora. His medical records were fully documented and up to date. The passport was

stamped by the British Horseracing Authority and his parent-
age was DNA tested and approved. This was the racehorse I had
dreamed of owning. Now, clutching his passport, it was literally
within my grasp.

Jenny remained unconvinced but she accepted the inevitability
of his coming. She knew how desperately disappointed I would
have been if he hadn't. And so, on Friday, May 21, 2010, in the late
morning, Adelphi Warrior arrived.

Mark and Alison pulled up with the trailer at our yard. They got
out cheerily and began to unfasten the side door. I was in a state of
nervous anticipation, a slightly sickly feeling in my stomach. Jenny
wanted to hide and pretend it wasn't ours.

News of our new acquisition had got round. Ladies at the yard
looked up from hefting barrows, haynets and buckets to see what
would emerge. We could see a long, orange head staring out from
within. Mark attached the headcollar and lead rope to it and began
to advance. Herman followed. He bounced athletically down the
ramp and clattered on to the road before standing still, drawing
himself up to his full height, snorting and looking around him at
his new surroundings.

'Oh my God,' said Jenny.

More heads craned round corners and jaws dropped at the
unnerving sight of Herman.

Clearly, people were thinking: 'What have they done now?'

The same thought was on our minds as we observed our new
horse. We had parted reluctantly with Baby in search of something
with a bit more spirit and athleticism. Herman seemed to have that
and more.

I looked on in awe as Mark brought him on to the yard and marched him into Baby's stable, carefully prepared with a big bed of straw and a net of fresh haylage. Mark slipped off the headcollar and the horse's travel boots and we watched as Herman began making anxious, bustling circuits of the stable, pausing now and again to dash to the door for a worried look outside. He kept on the move, his eyes wide and rolling, as he tried to take in his new home. I gazed in wonderment.

Herman had arrived with his saddle and bridle and a blue plastic crate of belongings, including the furry numnah and the gold fly rug and hat. We stored his stuff away, made sure he was comfortable and left him to his nervous pacing in the hope that he would soon settle in.

We waved Mark and Alison off, once again reassured that we had found the ideal owners for Baby. We watched as their vehicle drove away, pulling the now empty trailer.

My thoughts turned to what had been in it, the big, orange racehorse pacing round Baby's stable. My racehorse. Now I had got it, what was I going to do with it?

I looked over the stable door. Herman nibbled at his haynet, then continued his pacing. He looked at me out of the corner of his rolling eye, but did not meet my gaze. I wondered what to make of him. It was hard to know yet. He seemed worried, but that was understandable, having just arrived at a strange place. He was on his toes, but that too was to be expected. There was an air of vulnerability and pent-up emotion about him. I was getting a feeling of a soul in need. And I was entranced by him. Already, I felt that this was a horse I could bond with, that he could really and truly be my horse.

So I decided to give him a name. I didn't like the sound of Herman. There was nothing wrong with it, I just couldn't see myself calling him Herman. It reminded me of the old comic vampire from *The Munsters*. I wanted my own name for my own horse. I thought about his racing name, Adelphi Warrior. It sounded Greek. Indeed, Adelphi derives from a Greek word meaning 'brother'.

I like my ancient history and I have a book somewhere about the most famous Greek warrior of them all, who conquered Europe and Asia and rode into battle on his beloved horse, Bucephalus. He became known as 'The Great'. There could be only one name for my own 'great' horse. I called him Alexander.

14

Beginnings

The livery yard where we keep our horses, known locally as Pilling's, is situated in a rural oasis just outside Skipton. It nestles alongside the Leeds-Liverpool Canal, where colourful boats are moored and visitors enjoy pleasant walks for miles along the towpath and on to The Pennine Way. Opposite the yard is a row of idyllic stone cottages with picture-book gardens, and a café, formerly used by monks for stabling their horses.

The lane running past winds uphill to a traditional country pub, which looks down on the yard and the canal and across to the rolling fields where the horses graze. The pub is a happy haunt for us, where we can sit and admire the horses while enjoying a drink and a bite to eat. Many a visitor has been bewildered by Jenny's running commentary on our horses' movements in the fields: 'Daniel's gone behind a tree, now he's back out!' or: 'Look, Alexander's rolling ... no, he's just got up again!'

The tranquil setting, friendliness, and devoted care the horses receive mean the stables at Pilling's are always full. The yard has two main barns, where most of the horses are housed, and horseshoe-shaped accommodation at the front, facing on to the horse walker and looking out on the lane.

The Black Mare, Daniel and Baby originally took up residence in adjoining stables in the middle of the horseshoe. They were large, airy and comfortable and the horses were very content. Daniel and The Black Mare were next to each other, with a walled partition just low enough for them to look over. The Black Mare has always vigorously guarded the privacy of her boudoir and took great exception to Daniel peeping mischievously over the wall at her. Being slightly smaller, he could just perch his quivering chin on the top and seemed to take great delight in spying on the infuriated mare. But by the time she had charged, ears flat back, at the wall, the offending rolling eyes and twitching whiskers had vanished.

Pilling's has a trailer park, an all-weather school, a showjumping field, and a washing-off area in front of the horse walker. Our horses enjoy hours of entertainment observing their friends being soaped, scrubbed and hosed off.

A big bonus is the cross-country field, reached by crossing the hump-backed canal bridge and heading up Muddy Lane, a rutted track which more than lives up to its name.

The field has everything needed for cross-country schooling: large flat areas for canter work; a variety of rustic fences, including logs, drops, walls, ditches, ski jumps and a trakehner; and a long, sloping hill to gallop up. There is a steeplechase fence, bowed over the years by horses jumping through the top of the brush, and a swift, bubbling stream, running into a pool beneath a willow tree.

It is a great place to practise and has brought us hours of fun. It was to become a popular playground and workplace for Alexander. But it is also the scene of some of my most dramatic and painful falls. On one occasion Daniel managed to oust me twice in five minutes, first when he span away from a rising pheasant, and then, after I had remounted, when he ducked and swerved away from a wooden railed cross-country jump at the summit of the hill.

My first fall from Alexander was in there, along with two further spectacular launches from him that left me hobbling and out of action for weeks.

The turnout fields at Pilling's have names rooted in the farming tradition of the Marton Estate that owns the land. A hand-drawn map in the office cabin shows the layout of the network of fields and there are little magnetic strips with the name of each horse written on for customers to stick in the relevant spaces. The quaint names of the fields give the map the quality of a children's storybook. In the summer months, clusters of magnetic strips show happy herds grazing in Butter Bowl Croft, Back Of House Meadow and Hillside Pasture.

Alexander's summer field was to be the appropriately titled Top Of Hill, a large expanse of grassland with spectacular views across the Yorkshire Dales to Malham Cove. We did not know what to expect when we turned him out for the first time. Some sort of explosive reaction, I suppose. The reality was a little different.

Jenny led the leggy thoroughbred up the sloped stony track to his field, high above the livery yard. Walking at his shoulder, she was again struck by the huge, bony height of him. His rippling gold fly rug served only to emphasise his enormous size. He towered over her. Alexander marched purposefully along on the end of his lead rope. His walk was jaunty and he looked neither to the left nor the right, but focused on what was in front of him.

The word robotic sprang to mind again. It seemed that he had been programmed at the racing yard to get on with his job, whatever it was, and now he was naturally doing the same with us. He had been asked to walk up a hill, so he got on with it. Getting to the steeper bit near the top he increased his pace into a vigorous power walk. We feared the explosion was about to take place. But it didn't and we realised Alexander was merely attacking the hill at its hardest part. The programming, no doubt.

At the crest of the hill, there are gates into four fields. The geldings' meadow is the second on the left. Just inside the entrance is a water trough. A line of hawthorn trees marks the bottom boundary, providing shelter in the winter and a refuge from the flies in the summer. The field slopes skywards to a high point that commands magnificent views, before dipping out of sight down the other side of the hill to Muddy Lane.

Alexander waited politely while Jenny unfastened the gate. She led him inside and hastily turned him towards her to prevent him charging away. Horses are often keen to gallop off when they are turned out, especially if their friends are not in sight. Jenny was used to an exuberant Black Mare allowing her a split second to release the headcollar before dashing away. She feared she would get even less time with Alexander. Braced for a sudden movement, and anxious to avoid his flying back hooves, she deftly whipped off the headcollar and stepped back. But Alexander simply blinked and strolled to the water trough for a long drink before wandering off to graze close by.

It was an unexpectedly reserved reaction to his playground pasture, where he would be free to have fun and get all the exercise he wanted. But we were to learn that he is a remarkably laid-back horse for 99 per cent of the time. The other one per cent is altogether different.

I was itching to ride him again and couldn't wait to get him in from the field the next morning. Any fears we had of him coming to harm on his first night out were dispelled. He was unscathed and walked in obediently, picking his way carefully down the stony track. We were acutely aware that we would be on our own when I got on him this time. There would be no Mark with a firm hold of his head. How would Alexander react in this strange place, with new owners?

Of course, you are never really on your own with the Ladies at the Yard, a collective pseudonym for the more sensible women horse owners at Pilling's who prefer a steady hack down the lane to galloping at cross-country fences. The Ladies, always kind and considerate, are fascinated and appalled in equal measure by my somewhat gung-ho antics.

Word soon got round that I planned to ride Alexander. Before we knew it, we had half a dozen helpers. The nice thing was that they genuinely wanted to assist. While some people might have been eager to watch a disaster unfold, the Ladies were there solely to help things go smoothly.

Alexander was tacked up and led out of the main yard, past the café and round into the outdoor arena, where we were joined by our little posse of assistants. My heart started to beat a little faster but I told myself to keep calm. Any nerves from me would quickly communicate to the horse.

The mounting block, skilfully fashioned by one of the Ladies from plastic milk crates, was smoothly put in place next to Alexander. The Ladies gathered and quietly took up their positions for the big moment. Two were at his head, another was ready to hold the stirrup. Everything was being done calmly and deliberately so as not to cause Alexander any stress. So far it was working.

I gathered myself together and slowly stood next to him on the mounting block. I put my left foot in the stirrup and eased my right leg over his back and into the right stirrup, held firmly by a Lady. Words of reassurance were spoken quietly. There was no movement from Alexander.

The Ladies moved away, leaving me on my own with the horse. He was still calm. I gave him the gentlest of squeezes to his sides with my lower leg. Instantly, he moved forward into a steady but purposeful walk and we began to circle the school. I deliberately rode him on a long rein so I wasn't pulling on his mouth. It meant I had less control but the plan was to settle him. The more relaxed I was, the more likely he would be to relax. I didn't want him to get tense and kick off.

The tactic was going well. We walked round the outside of the school, changing the rein to go in a different direction, and then adopting smaller circles. Alexander walked gently forward and his head started to drop as his body relaxed.

'He's so chilled with you already,' said one of the Ladies.

After 15 minutes we came out of the school. It couldn't have been a better start. The next question was when to stop. How far should

I push this first ride? Because things were going so well I decided to walk him down the lane. This was more risky. With nothing to confine him, if he suddenly took off I could be in trouble.

Again, his behaviour could not be faulted. He walked out positively, with that same bouncy gait that had so excited me the first time, but there was not a hint of rebellion.

We crossed the canal bridge and followed the lane as it wound between the trees until the bottom of the cross-country field came into view. Alexander's attention was caught by the sweeping green vista to our right, rustic fences dotted around it. But we carried on walking calmly down the lane.

Where the cross-country field ends, the lane swings left and climbs uphill away from it. In the corner, before the hill, is a gate that leads into the field. It opens on to a narrow grassy path that follows the left-hand edge of the stream. Across the shallow water, the field opens out and stretches away magnificently all the way up to the top end of Muddy Lane.

My courage was up. I pointed Alexander to the right and went through the gate. Instantly, there was an extra spring in his step. We walked down the grass track and reached the stream. It is a couple of feet wide at this point, with a stony bed that the water cascades noisily over before flowing into a deeper and wider pool. The crossing point is only a few inches deep but it can terrify young and inexperienced horses. Alexander did not seem to be particularly worried so I sat tight and squeezed him with my legs. He looked down but ploughed into the water and out the other side.

Now we were in the field proper. It looked bigger and wider than it had ever done. There was plenty of space for a thoroughbred racehorse to run wild. This was the moment of truth. There was no going back now. I was about to find out if I could survive in here on Alexander. Would I have any control? I pointed him towards the bottom of the field, reasoning he would soon run out of room if he took off with me, and, hopefully, stop. We began to trot and I waited, my heart in my mouth, for him to burst into action. Nothing happened. We continued trotting.

Astonished, I gave him a squeeze and asked him to canter. Again, I prepared for an explosion. Again, it did not happen. I found myself cantering very steadily round in a circle at the bottom of the field. 'This is ridiculous,' I thought. 'It's supposed to be a racehorse.'

Feeling confident, I decided to take on the ultimate test. 'To hell with it,' I reasoned. 'I might as well find out now if it's going to kill me.' I pointed Alexander at the hill, sloping steeply up to the top of the field, the place where we always ran our horses, the fun bit. But was I looking for trouble by asking Alexander to gallop?

This time I got a response. A sudden surge of power thrust me forward and he was off. In an instant he had gone up several gears. It was as if he was back on the racecourse. We were hurtling along, much quicker than I had ever been taken before. He was eating up the ground. And yet, despite the speed, I felt secure. He seemed to glide across the grass, so rhythmic was his movement. I had eased myself out of the saddle, crouching slightly forward in a poor imitation of a jockey. But it felt comfortable and the position seemed to give Alexander confidence. It was what he was used to.

We were halfway up the hill when another thought struck me. Would I have any brakes? Could I stop him at the top of the hill, like the other horses? Or would he go hurtling over the boundary fence? Fearing to unsettle him by tugging drastically, I gently eased back the reins. Immediately, his pace slackened. Gradually we went down the gears until, neatly inside the perimeter of the field, we came to a bouncy stop. The brakes had worked perfectly.

We stood for a few moments at the top of the hill, Alexander puffing slightly from his exertions. He shook his head in appreciation of the exciting gallop. Sitting astride my prancing chestnut steed, I gazed at the magnificent view across the rolling hills and wondered if life could get any better. 'This is the life, eh, Alexander? I think you're going to enjoy it here,' I said. Alexander snorted enthusiastically.

I was on cloud nine as we marched down Muddy Lane and back to the yard. The ride had gone perfectly. But not everything went so smoothly in the days after Alexander's arrival. Letting rip in the cross-country field was obviously a highlight for him. It was a release of nervous energy. But within the confines of the stableyard there were very clear signs that all was not well in his world.

Daniel and The Black Mare would constantly hang their heads over their stable doors to watch what was happening. By contrast, Alexander hid at the back of his box, peeping out at us from beneath his orange fringe and declining to venture forward, despite our encouragements. He seemed frightened about what the world outside might have to offer him.

'Look, it's plotting to kill us,' Jenny would say, still deeply suspicious of the new arrival, lurking monster-like in the depths.

Once we had put the headcollar on him, he obediently walked out of his stable but we soon found that was the extent of his willingness. Tacked up, he was quite happy to do what we wanted.

But without the saddle and bridle on, there were major issues and concerns. He would not do the simple things that are part and parcel of the day-to-day management and exercise of a horse.

When we brought him in from the field he refused to go on to the wash area slats to have the mud cleaned off his legs. He dug his toes in and bounced backwards. He was not alone in being reluctant about the slats, but a large, athletic Alexander beating a hasty retreat was a worrying sight for everyone.

It added to the theory on the yard, politely put, that my new horse was 'a big step up'.

The sound of cascading water from the hidden depths below the concrete slats can be unnerving. But the sight of Alexander sidestepping round puddles on the yard, rather than getting his toes wet, was unexpected.

More surprisingly, he would not go on the horse walker. These are essential on racing yards as a means of getting the horses fit, so we knew he must have used them before. I could not understand why he would not go near ours. This was a major concern. In the worst of the winter weather it is often the only way to exercise a horse. What would happen in those cold, dark months if we couldn't get him on the walker? We could end up with an unexercised ex-racehorse, so frustrated he would be uncontrollable.

I hadn't given much thought to the management of Alexander before he arrived. I relied on Jenny's better knowledge of horses, and anyway I was too excited about getting him. But these were worrying difficulties needing serious consideration.

I was beginning to get a picture of Alexander as a four-legged person, rather than simply an athlete. The picture was one of vulnerability. Looking into his eyes, I could see worry and fear and uncertainty. Something had happened to make him afraid. That didn't mean anyone had been cruel to him, far from it. Physically he was in good condition and in the few weeks he had been with Mark and Alison, he was shown every kindness.

But he was a lost soul. Perhaps the racing world had not suited him. Maybe it was just that he had been moved to different places in a relatively short space of time and hadn't had the chance to get close to anyone for long enough. Now he was at another new home and did not know what was going to happen next.

He needed a person to love and trust: someone who would love and trust him in return. The last thing he needed was someone to fight with him. That would be disastrous. It would signal the end of our relationship with him and put his future in grave doubt. He had already blown his chance with Mark. He wouldn't get another one.

The answer was to win him over, to gain his trust and his confidence, and through that, his love. Instead of trying to bully and force him on to the walker or the slats, we tried gentle encouragement and kind words. And if he had to have dirty legs for a little while, then so be it.

I made it my personal crusade. I was determined that we would bond. I wanted to be the one to help him, the one he would trust and love. Each day I spent time with him, talking to him and brushing him. Then, I would walk him towards the slats or the walker. We stood and watched other horses being washed down, or revolving on the walker, while I quietly explained to him what was happening and reassured him that nothing nasty would befall him.

He stood with me and took it all in. When he looked at me I could see the fear starting to fade from his eyes. Perhaps he was beginning to trust me. And then, a week or so into the process, he went with me and walked on to the slats and we stood together looking at the water below. It was a magical moment. For the first time I felt there was some sort of union between us.

The next day I took him across to the horse walker. We stood near the entrance and I opened the metal door with my left hand, holding him by his lead rope with my right. No other horse was on it and the metallic contraption was motionless. The weather was kind, with no wind or rain. We faced the empty space where the door had been.

'Do you want a closer look?' I said, and we moved forward on to the shallow step on the very edge of the walker. Alexander stood, his long, orange nose with its crooked white blaze actually inside the horse walker. This was as near as we had got. Now we had forward momentum I felt the opportunity was there. I clicked my tongue in encouragement and said quietly, 'Come on, then,' and, without tugging, put some gentle pressure on the lead rope. I felt him relax his body and begin to move. Suddenly, we were standing in one of the walker's compartments.

'Good boy, good boy,' I praised, patting and stroking his neck. His body language suggested he had accepted being on the walker. But there was still uncertainty in his eye. He was trusting me but I felt he needed to trust a little bit more.

'Close the door,' I said to Jenny.

'What?' The tone of her voice and the look of disbelief told me she was unhappy with what I was planning.

'Close the door,' I repeated firmly. The door clanged into place, leaving Alexander and I enclosed together inside.

'Turn it on. Keep it at a slow speed,' I instructed.

Jenny did as I asked. The walker began to move. I clicked again and told Alexander to walk on. Linked together by the lead rope, like an umbilical cord, we shuffled forward and began revolving slowly with the walker. This was not a concept taken from any health and safety manual. In fact, it flew in the face of common sense. The metal sides of the walker, and the compartment dividers, are eight feet high. There was no way out, for the horse or for me.

I was taking a big risk. I was trapped. If Alexander panicked and reared or kicked out in that confined space I could be seriously injured. And no one could get to me quickly or easily. But I was prepared to take the risk. Alexander needed me and I was going to be there for him. If I could get him over his walker phobia it would be a massive stride forward, for him and for us. This was not a view shared by The Boss when he happened upon us setting out on our second circuit.

Tim Pilling – or The Boss – runs the livery yard business with his wife, Sheila. Tim is burly with a mop of blond curls and cuts a distinctive and imposing figure. He is rarely seen without his trademark checked lumberjack shirts and rolled-up fag perched in the corner of his mouth, and he is never happier than when trundling about performing some agricultural task on one of his treasured tractors and diggers.

Tim is blunt speaking but honest and warm hearted. With his strength, tenacity and practicality, he is just the man when his customers have a crisis. Many was the time we had to thank him for bodily hefting a defiant and mulish Baby into the trailer. His own health and safety are not at the top of his list of priorities and he has an unorthodox, devil-may-care way of doing things. He was left nursing a badly bruised bottom when he climbed to the top of the straw trailer to deliver a hearty kick to a wedged bale, only to slip on the moss on top of the shed wall and plummet to the floor. As a customer, you know where you stand and if you are fair with him, you will be well looked after. On the other hand, if you cheat him or don't pay your bills, you'll be, rightly, on your bike.

Tim is a farmer not an equestrian, and though he can ride, he doesn't bother. But he understands horses and has a way of making them bow to his will, using a combination of strength, determination and kindness. He never once hit Baby, he just kept on tugging the static chap to wherever he needed to go. And he once pulled an elderly retired racehorse out of the canal after it tumbled in from its summer pasture.

He has a quiet admiration for those of us who go out and compete. He may not say it in so many words, but I reckon he is quite proud when people from the yard come back with a handful of hard-earned rosettes. Tim is very laid-back. It takes a lot to make him cross. But now he was very cross.

'What the bloody hell is he doing?' he demanded. 'He's going to kill himself. Get him off there.' The walker came to a stop and I emerged sheepishly. The Boss shook his curly head in exasperation before stomping off.

But I had achieved my aim. Alexander was settled and I stood next to the metal grille, proudly watching as he walked round on his own. After half a dozen circuits we switched off the walker and

I led him back to his stable. He looked pleased with himself. I was delighted. I had put my faith in him and he had rewarded me with his trust.

With that bridge crossed, we could look to the next challenge.

15

Getting To Know You

My dream of having my own racehorse had, out of the blue, become a reality. But the reality of riding Alexander would be very different from the dream. We would have to go back to basics to turn him from what he was, into what I wanted him to be, into something that I could cope with.

Nevertheless, my brain was buzzing with the excitement of owning such a creature. A whole new chapter of life had suddenly opened up. Looking at him, anything seemed possible: The Grand National, Badminton Horse Trials? The sky was the limit. All I needed to do was adapt in order to handle the extreme athlete I had acquired. It was, of course, a very big 'all'.

Alexander was at least 16.3 hands high, touching on 17 hands, far taller than any of our other horses. He was muscular but very lean and had an energy about him that I was going to have to get used to.

Ten days after his arrival, we went on our first outing, to the family's favourite cross-country training ground, Craven Country

Ride. The Spring Bank Holiday Trail Ride seemed the ideal opportunity to get to know him. I crammed in as much riding as I could in preparation; cantering up the cross-country field and quietly hacking down the lane, both alone and in company. What surprised me was the control I was able to assert over Alexander at this early stage and how ready he was to go at the pace I wanted.

We had encountered stubbornness and uncertainty from him around the yard, but once I was on him and had set off, he almost literally seemed to breathe a sigh of relief and become happier and more relaxed. There was no hint of the powerful outbursts to come.

We were accompanied to Craven Country Ride by Jenny on The Black Mare and my daughter Sophie on Daniel. We hacked over, steadily and uneventfully, but when we arrived at the spectacular countryside venue and Alexander caught sight of the rolling grassy fields and rustic jumps, he seemed to grow. There was an anticipation and a simmering excitement about him. I shared his feelings but I also felt the nerves building. This was a very big test for me, although I still did not appreciate just what I had taken on.

As we entered the first field, a line of flagged fences came into view and Alexander began sweating and jogging. He was itching to go but was polite enough to wait for me. When I released him and we cantered, I found I was still in control. We bowled across the field, steering well clear of the fences, and successfully pulled up at the far end. First test passed.

The next field offered a small and inviting log. I let the others hop over it first. Alexander's eyes were on stalks, impatiently watching his companions jumping and more than ready to join in. He tugged at the reins and I walked him in a circle, preparing for the moment. Jenny and Sophie pulled up ahead of the fence and maintained a protective guard on either side, a reassuring sight.

As eager as my horse, I turned towards the log and let him go. He was keen and bounded towards the fence. I concentrated on sitting quietly and keeping my balance, squeezing my lower leg around him and thrusting my heels down. He sprang over the 18-inch jump, giving it at least the same height in clearance. We landed together and Alexander excitedly cantered past the others towards an uphill slope. But as soon as I asked him to slow down and pull up, he did. The discipline of his racing training was still very clear in his head.

We turned, walked back and jumped the log again, this time more sensibly, and pulled up once more. Alexander was snorting and shaking his head, loving the little jump and canter, but I felt in control. This was great fun.

The three of us carried on around the trail, walking and trotting, having the occasional controlled canter and popping a few small and simple obstacles. Alexander even went happily into the big water complex, wading and splashing without alarm.

All went without a hiccup until we stopped for homemade cake and fruit punch, a traditional treat served up to the riders halfway round the trail. Alexander was enjoying himself so much he did not want to stop. Our five-minute break became an ordeal for everyone else as he refused to stand still. I just managed to drink the contents of my little plastic cup but Sophie had no such luck. My impatient steed suddenly began reversing at speed, barging into an indignant Daniel and squashing him against a gate. Sophie's complimentary fruit punch was spilled everywhere. We hurriedly moved on.

The rest of the ride passed smoothly and we hacked slowly back home. It had gone remarkably well. Alexander's behaviour had, for the most part, been very impressive. It was an encouraging start.

Over the next couple of weeks, Alexander relaxed even more. The stress and worry that seemed to engulf him after he arrived largely disappeared. He went from explosively edgy to suspiciously chilled out. Increasingly, he was to be found lying snoozing in his stable. I was convinced that he was the horse of my dreams – my dream chaser. He was still on trial with us, as was Baby with Mark and Alison. But we knew they wanted to keep him so, in mid-June, I drove up to South Lakeland to complete the deal.

Mark and I exchanged horse passports and shook hands. Alexander was mine. I finally had my racehorse. But the day was tinged with sadness. Baby Horse, for all his stubbornness and eccentricities, had been a much-loved member of the family. Jenny bought him for £300 when he was a shaggy, cinnamon-coloured yearling, limping painfully round the field with his brother, after tearing his back leg in wire.

It was a wonderful move for him, with new owners who loved him and would attend to his every need. But this was goodbye. As I drove away, I deliberately took a winding route along a narrow lane that allowed me to crane my neck to peer at Baby's ginger back, slowly fading into the distance as he grazed in the meadow that was now his home. As I came to the final bend that would take him out of sight, I stopped the car and got out. I gazed back for a last lingering glimpse.

The tears that had been welling up, fell from my eyes. At last, I turned away, got back in the car and drove off. It was time to head home, where my racehorse awaited.

16

Rider On The Storm

I knew very little about Alexander's background but I made it my mission to find out as much as I could about him. He was just six years old and his passport told me that his dad was called Alflora, his mum was Gun Shot and her dad, Alexander's grandad, was Gunner B. A cursory look at the *Racing Post* website told me that Alflora had finished sixth in the 1992 Epsom Derby and Gun Shot had won three races over hurdles, while Gunner B had won 15 races on the Flat in the 1970s. Alexander's breeding was impressive but beyond that I was in the dark. He looked like an athlete and he felt like an athlete to me. But how good was he and how good might he become?

I knew someone qualified to try to answer that. And when we bumped into Keith Rosier at a local show, I asked him to come and ride Alexander later that day. Keith arrived with his hat and boots and got on my horse. Fascinated, I followed them into the cross-country field and watched from the top as they smoothly cantered around. After a while, the pair moved into the showjumping field and popped over some small crossbars. When they trotted back to me, Keith was grinning from ear to ear. He simply said: 'It's well good.'

That gave me all the answers I needed.

Alexander was becoming so laid-back it was hard to imagine him galloping round a racecourse jumping 4ft 6ins steeplechase fences, as he had been doing just a few months before, or landing his former owner in hospital. Mark could only recall the horse rearing up before he came round in the local infirmary. But I was about to get a couple of reminders of what Alexander was capable of. On the horizon, the storm clouds were gathering.

Worried that my ex-racehorse was getting a little on the sleepy side, I decided to use up Baby's leftover oats in his suppers. Not the smartest of moves. While oats are ideal for giving a bit of vim to a lazy, lumbering chap like Baby, they are rocket fuel to a young, fit thoroughbred like Alexander, as I was to find to my cost.

I confidently took him into the cross-country field and, after a canter round, put him at a little rustic fence. It was the first time we had jumped in there and the excitement was too much for him. We sailed over and as he landed he bucked, twisted in the air, and bucked again. I hit the ground hard and bounced while Alexander, showing more dash in four seconds than he had in the previous four weeks, hurtled riderless up the meadow.

It was my first fall from Alexander and it was a lot different from falling off Daniel. I almost slid off Daniel, and it wasn't far to the ground. With Alexander, not only did I have further to fall, but because of his speed, power and agility, I was launched with greater velocity. And it happened so quickly I was hitting the ground before I had the chance to think about it, let alone do anything to stop it.

I stayed down for a few seconds, slightly stunned, then got to my feet. My hat silk and whip were yards away but, apart from bruises and a minor finger injury, I was unscathed – and undaunted. Impressed by my horse's athleticism, I limped back to the yard and announced: 'If Keith can get bucked off, so can I.' His horse, Black Jack, had recently launched him in the collecting ring at an event.

Soon afterwards, we saw the stressy racing side of Alexander in all its dubious glory. We decided to buy our own tack for him. One of the best saddlers we know is Todds of Kendal and they had a trade stand at Skipton Horse Trials at the end of June. The trials are the most prestigious riding event in the area and top professionals such as Oliver Townend have competed there. Keith is a regular competitor, and Esme and The Black Mare had one of their finest hours at Skipton when they finished ninth in the Intro class. I had the honour of leading in the horse, white with sweat and magnificently triumphant, after her fast, clear cross-country round secured their top ten finish.

We took Alexander to the horse trials so he could have a personal saddle fitting from the experts at Todds. Although we went towards the end of the day, when most riders had finished competing, the parking area was still dotted with horseboxes and trailers and there were beautifully manicured equine athletes everywhere. With the crowds and blaring commentary, Alexander must have thought he was back at the races. His long neck grew alarmingly as he craned out of the side door of The Boss's trailer. His eyes rolled, his nostrils flared and he neighed shudderingly and repeatedly while booting the trailer.

He was a frightening sight and Jenny anxiously sought help from our friend David Elms, who had been competing, to hang on to Alexander's headcollar while the saddle fitting took place. David then loaded Alexander back into the trailer and we took him home. He arrived back lathered in sweat but calmed down in his stable and, after a hearty tea, trotted off up his field.

It was an eye-opener for us. At the time, we thought he must have been excited by the racing scenario and frustrated that he was not taking part. Now we know more about him and his uncertainty over racing, it seems likely his outburst at Skipton arose from anxiety.

What we did not know at the time was that he had been racing only a matter of weeks before he came to us. No wonder he kicked off so badly. Not all horses take to racing. Many love it, but others simply don't enjoy the barging and buffeting in a big race field. Alexander, despite his athleticism, was one of the latter. He can still get nervous when he is squeezed for space by other horses.

Right now, he was happy to potter about with us, gaining cross-country confidence with trips to Craven Country Ride, before tackling his first event – a challenging 1ft Clear Round competition!

The occasional Clear Round contests at our yard are a bit of Sunday morning fun. The idea is to get as many people involved as possible, from the serious competitors to the happy hackers. The courses are tiny to begin with for the less confident and those who rarely jump, building up to greater heights for the brave few. There is a plentiful supply of rosettes and the day is one of camaraderie rather than intense competition.

It seemed a nice way to begin Alexander's competitive career with us. He was very relaxed as we tacked him up and took him to the showjumping field. It was a fine summer day, but not too hot, and Alexander snoozed in the sun as he waited in a line of sleepy horses for his turn in the smallest class.

His puzzled expression was a picture as he was trotted by a brave Esme towards the first tiny cross-pole. Here was an ex-steeplechaser who, only that spring, had been jumping huge fences at a full gallop. He had probably never seen a showjumping obstacle before, let alone one so small. The tall, leggy chap was no doubt having difficulty seeing what he was supposed to jump over.

Alexander may have been bewildered but he was unfazed by the gentle task we had provided him with. He obediently popped round the course, naturally springing high over the seven little jumps, before returning to the line to sunbathe again. Jenny was overjoyed when he was presented with his first rosette, a light blue ribbon for going clear.

Now he was warmed up, I took him in the 2ft class, where he was more fluent. He clearly found the bigger fences a lot more comfortable and he seemed to enjoy himself as we cantered round. A pink rosette was our reward this time.

'Are you man enough for a pink ribbon?' asked one of the Ladies. On my tall steeplechaser I felt man enough for anything!

Jenny had treated me to orange rubber 'racing reins', ordered over the internet, and Alexander's new bridle had the blingiest gold metal browband she felt I would allow.

Long, lean and muscular, he would not have looked out of place being led round at the start of the Grand National. His red tail was trimmed short and the athletic grooved 'racing lines' on his flanks marked him out as a trained racer.

We followed the family's golden rule of always trying to end on a positive note, and left the Clear Round event at that. With Daniel and The Black Mare winning a clutch of rosettes, it had been a good day.

It had certainly gone better than the first time I took Alexander into the showjumping field. A couple of weeks earlier, I arranged a lesson in there with David Elms, who played a key role in training us in those early stages. As we walked up Muddy Lane to the entrance gate, something upset Alexander.

In the next field a Le Trec event was taking place. Le Trec is a horse sport combining orienteering with tricky obstacle negotiation. There was a good turnout for the event. Competitors' wagons and trailers were parked around the field and an old white commentary box had been positioned next to the fence enclosing the showjumping field. I suspect it was this that alarmed Alexander. Turning in to the gate, he stopped and went into reverse gear. I found we were suddenly going backwards down Muddy Lane at increasing speed. We were later to learn that reversing was a tactic Alexander had used before when he did not want to do something.

David, in very firm tones, told me to take action. If Alexander was allowed to get away with it, we would be creating big trouble for the future. I managed to halt his backward progress but could not make him move forward. Then he started to step back again.

I stopped him for a second time and, with determination and a strong leg, I began to inch him forward. The gate – and the commentary box – slowly came back into view. Alexander was still trying to wriggle out of it but I managed to hold him in position and, with a final squeeze of the leg, I got him into the field.

David was full of praise and, indeed, I had won a significant victory. I had proved to myself, and to Alexander, that if there was a battle to be had it was possible for me to win it. My aim was to keep winning them, but some I would comprehensively lose, and another commentary box would be central to a dramatic episode when we started seriously competing.

In those early weeks I was to witness at first hand what it was like to fight a battle with Alexander. This time, David was in the saddle. He was helping with Alexander's schooling and was so impressed with him, he told me: 'If you let me have him for two years, I think I could get him to Badminton.'

He was less enthusiastic after he was left hobbling when the pair had a terrible fall-out in the school. David is a strong rider and he is used to getting his way with horses when they disagree about how to do things. But a young Alexander was still backward-thinking and stubborn and he was keen to do things his way. David was trying to help the horse to use his body properly. He was working hard and he expected Alexander to do the same.

Alexander had other ideas. The more David tried to get him to do what he wanted, the more angry and frustrated Alexander became. He can roll his eyes wildly and it is a clear warning that trouble is afoot. He was not used to schooling and he did not want to do it. Now he was being made to work, the eye rolling was going into overdrive. He was simmering and the explosion was not long in coming.

Alexander started to throw his head from side to side, then he shook his body and began to rear. He had had enough and it was clear he was trying to bring the schooling to an end by removing David, who was having none of it. It takes a lot to dislodge David and his failure to do so made Alexander more angry. And the angrier he got, the more determined David got.

I watched from outside the school as the battle grew more intense. It was enthralling and terrifying at the same time. I wondered how I would cope in the same circumstances but quickly put the uncomfortable thought out of my head. At last the war ended. Alexander, now tired, admitted defeat but not before he had deliberately rammed David into the fence, leaving him bruised and sore.

The incident brought home to me that falling out with Alexander was to be avoided. The best way for me to ride him was quietly but positively. If he needed to be disciplined, I had to find a subtle way of doing it without him realising.

While Alexander was unenthusiastic about his schooling, my cross-country dream remained firmly intact. All the signs pointed to him being a natural cross-country horse. He certainly had the speed and fitness, as The Black Mare found out one day when she and Alexander galloped together up the cross-country field. It was annoying enough for her to be made to set off behind Alexander, as she was used to leading the way up the hill. But when her best efforts failed to catch the thoroughbred, she was furious. She reached the top in a strop, hanging out her tongue and tossing her head indignantly. Alexander was scarcely puffing.

As the summer progressed, Alexander learned to jump in and out of water and leap modest logs, banks and ditches with confidence. Literally, he took everything in his stride, almost always meeting the fences perfectly. When his stride wasn't spot on he was quick to put it right, usually with an extra short stride, or sometimes standing off the fence to jump.

It was all going well, too well as it turned out, and I was to come down to earth with two very big bumps on our next trip to Craven Country Ride. Just days after we had praised him for being 'almost too good to be true', Alexander dropped me twice in a few minutes. In fairness, neither fall could be blamed on him. His athleticism when jumping could prove too much for me at this stage.

The first fall came as we tackled a line of fences of different types, and it was the first sign of uncertainties to come. I wasn't expecting him to have any problems with a spruce fence, a smaller version of the steeplechase jumps he had been used to. But as we approached it, he became anxious and, as we took off, he veered violently to the left. I flew over his left shoulder and landed with a thump.

Alexander raced off, hotly pursued by Sophie on Daniel. He charged to the end of the field but then ran out of ideas and began to worry about being in the countryside on his own. Spotting the reassuring sight of Daniel, he allowed himself to be caught and returned to his rider.

I was in one piece and I knew I had to get straight back on. If I did not brave it now, I might not have the courage to gallop and jump him again. Reunited, we safely tackled a few small logs and I felt my confidence returning.

During the afternoon, we added some new fences to our list, including straw bales, a roll-top in the water and a daunting hanging log. One last challenge remained, a chunky brush fence. If I could pilot Alexander over that it would be another successful day and I could forget about the fall.

As we cantered into the jump my confidence wavered. It was bigger than I had thought. But I was committed now. Perhaps my anxiety communicated itself to Alexander. Or maybe he just got overexcited. Either way, he took an exuberant leap over the fence and threw in an athletic twist on landing. And that was that. I was on the deck again and Alexander was legging it up the hill with his reins flapping. It was like the old days with Daniel, but much more spectacular.

I knelt on the ground, shaken and nursing a scraped arm and a bruised back, while Sophie and Daniel repeated their earlier cowboy act. This was not what I had planned.

When Jenny, who was at work, rang to find out how we were doing, it was Sophie who answered my phone.

'Yes,' she cheerily replied. 'We're fine. Dad's fallen off twice but we've had a good day.' Jenny nearly fell off her chair.

I was now having doubts. Maybe it had been a big mistake to get Alexander. Maybe he was just too much for me. Even David Coates, who runs the Craven Country Ride, was concerned, especially after another horseman commented: 'That man on the chestnut's a resilient bugger. It's already come past twice without him!'

'Rome wasn't built in a day,' David advised me.

In other words: 'Don't be so bloody silly next time.'

David was right. Perhaps I was rushing things. The excitement at getting Alexander had got the better of me. You have to take your time to adapt to a horse like him. I was literally going too fast. But soon I would be forced to take it much steadier. And Alexander would suffer an injury so serious that his whole future was at stake.

17

Broken Dream

Alexander had been with us for three months when the physiotherapist paid a routine visit to the yard. Although he had been lightly raced, the jumping and galloping can put a strain on the horses' backs and legs, so it seemed like a good idea to get him checked out.

The physio examined him thoroughly and found no problems with his back but when she moved to his legs the prognosis was different. She discovered a weak tendon in his near hind leg. It was not a long-term injury but it needed sorting out or it could become one. The remedy was to build up the tendon by walking for two months. I would be able to ride him, but at no more than a walk during the whole two-month period. Just as I was striving to adapt to his athleticism and gain confidence I was going to be severely restricted in what I could do with him.

The August Bank Holiday Trail Ride at Craven Country Ride was out of the window, along with any competing. We were back to square one, and after two months I would still have to be patient and slowly build up Alexander's level of work. It was terribly frustrating. I was coming to a virtual halt before I had fully got into my stride. But perhaps it was just what I needed. And Alexander seemed perfectly happy to be just walking. If he was fed up he didn't show it.

The weeks dragged for me. I wanted to gallop him up the cross-country field, but at least the leisurely hacks out were helping to bring us together. The gentle pace relaxed Alexander and gave me the chance to reflect more about the person behind the four-legged athlete. I did not yet fully understand Alexander. He was a cool customer and didn't give much away about what he was thinking and feeling. He didn't wear his heart on his sleeve, as Daniel did, but he was restful to be with and the fact that he seemed happy in his life with us was gratifying.

I thought about my feelings towards him. It was a subtle process, falling in love with a horse like him. He didn't demand to be loved, like Daniel. But his fragility and vulnerability drew you in. I wanted to wrap my arms around his long, orange neck and give him a hug, so I did. His response was neither to object, nor to welcome the hugs, but simply to accept them.

The weeks went slowly, but they were passing. A month had gone by. Just one more month of walking to go.

Tuesday, September 28, 2010, ten days after my 52nd birthday, is etched in my memory. I was walking along the platform at Leeds railway station after covering a case at the city's Crown Court when I got the phone call from Jenny. It was hard to hear what she was saying above the hubbub of commuters and noisy station announcements. But what was all too clear was the awful upset and panic in her voice. And then her words registered: 'Alexander's been badly injured.'

Jenny had been contacted by The Boss. That meant it was serious. It was so serious they had decided not to move Alexander until the vet, who was summoned at once, reached him. All we knew was that he had put his near hind leg, the one with the weak tendon, through the post and rail fence in the field, dragged it out and cut it badly. How badly was not clear, but his blood was everywhere and he was standing next to the fence on three legs. The rest of the herd had kept their distance, except for Daniel, who had become unexpectedly close to the thoroughbred. He had stayed protectively at his side.

The vet was on her way. Until then we could only guess horribly about how this might end.

I carried on with my journey in a complete whirl. Suddenly, nothing mattered but Alexander's well-being. I felt sick to the stomach, as if I had been poisoned. My pride and joy was wounded, potentially fatally. Horses have strong but delicate legs and there is a limit to what can be done to repair them. Medical and techno-logical advances and veterinary skills have pushed out the recovery boundaries. But there are still too many sad cases where nothing can be done and the only humane course is to have the horse put down.

Now, facing that possibility, my mind was clear about exactly how much Alexander meant to me. He was everything. I was dis-traught. Things were made worse by my feeling of utter helpless-ness. I was 30 miles away. My car was halfway up the railway line to home and it would take up to two hours to get back to the yard. There was nothing I could do but wait for news. But I knew that when the next phone call came, it might be to tell me that Alexander was dead.

When the phone rang, it brought me hope. The vet had examined Alexander, bandaged his leg and led him down from the field. The Boss had loaded him into his trailer and driven him to the horse hospital. The fact that Alexander had been able to walk to the trailer was massively good news. He had got over the first huge hurdle. The injury was not so bad that he had needed to be put down where he was. Now I could start to think in terms of his recovery, however long it might take.

Buoyed by these positive thoughts, we went to the yard to give the ever-hungry Daniel his supper. After tucking him in for the night we headed for the sanctuary of our little cottage. As we drove past the pub we saw The Boss's Land Rover parked outside. It was the excuse we needed. In we went to hear a first-hand account of Alexander's accident, while soothing our souls with a much-needed whisky.

It had been an awful few hours but Alexander was alive. Now all I wanted was to see him. It was too late to go that day. Hospital visiting hours were long over and the patients would be settled for the night. I would have to wait until I got through the next day in the office.

Work dragged but at last we were able to leave Bradford and make our way to the well-respected equine clinic at Rathmell, near Settle. We had been there before, with Baby Horse. In March 2009, we had him admitted for tests on his soundness, airways and eyesight. When Baby arrived he was confronted by the sight of an equine patient taking a dip in the hydrotherapy pool. Baby boggled in consternation and refused to budge as the mare paddled energetically around, snorting loudly. We finally coaxed him into the building and settled him into a stable with a pool view.

He was diagnosed with inflammation of the lungs and returned home with a medicinal inhaler that had to be administered by covering one nostril and clamping a plastic respirator over the other. At first, Baby had to be pinned in a corner of his stable to give him the medicine but he quickly began to look forward to his next fix of happy gas.

He was then prescribed Ventipulmin Granules, to be mixed with his feed, and survived an accidental massive overdose by Jenny who gave him 20 scoops instead of the recommended dose of two. The next morning, Baby's Easter bonnet was slightly askew and he had sweated in the night but he was otherwise unharmed, his mad amber eyes gleaming and his gingerish coat shining with well-being. It added weight to our theory that he might be an alien!

Alexander was in the same stable with the poolside view that Baby had occupied. He was munching at a pile of hay in the corner. His injured leg was encased in a large red bandage but he seemed at ease and he was moving round well.

'Now then, lad. How are you?' I asked cheerily. He peered round at me and carried on eating. Not so bad, it seemed.

With the hospital staff about to do their evening rounds, we had only a few minutes to spend with Alexander. But we were allowed to give him a couple of small treats and we left feeling reassured that he was settled and comfortable.

At the weekend we were able to go for a longer visit to Rathmell. Our timing was perfect. Just as we reached Alexander's stable, the vet arrived to change his bandage. We walked steadily with Alexander to the examination room, around the edge of the pool. Unlike Baby, he did not give it a second glance.

Alexander was sedated before the bandage was changed. I stood holding his headcollar, ready to support him. As the drug began to take effect, his head started to sink until his chin rested on my chest. His eyes were glazing over and occasionally his head jerked as he tried to stay awake, like a little old man nodding off in his chair in front of the fire. For me, it was a tender few moments. He was so large and yet so fragile, but I was there for him. We stood with our heads together and I couldn't have felt closer to him.

When the bandage was removed we saw the injury for the first time. The skin and flesh at the front of his near hind leg, just below the hock joint, had been ripped away, cutting him to the bone and slicing through his extensor tendon. It had left a gaping wound, which had been cleaned and bandaged, and he had been given antibiotics and painkillers.

It was obviously a very serious injury. Alexander had survived it but we were unclear about the healing process and about his future prospects. While the vet seemed happy with the wound, and the x-rays of it, he remained non-committal about Alexander's long-term recovery. When things are uncertain, a vet has to be cautious and not over-optimistic.

Alexander began to come round from his sedative and our magical few minutes of togetherness came to an end. I led him slowly back to his spotless stable and we left the nursing staff to their jobs.

We visited again on the Sunday and I took some photos on my phone of the bandaged, but cosy, Alexander in his stable. Now we looked forward to getting him home where we could nurse him ourselves in a familiar environment.

After eight days, the go-ahead was given for him to leave hospital. We were at work and The Boss stepped in once more to take on the role of ambulance driver. It was uplifting to see Alexander when we got to the yard. He seemed happy to show off his large, bright red bandage, peering round as if to admire it.

Vet Joe McKinder was in charge of Alexander's care. He is thorough and has a relaxed and caring approach to his patients. I knew my horse was in good hands. Joe visited Alexander regularly and at first he was pleased with his progress. But after several days there was no sign of the wound knitting together. The healing process seemed to have stalled.

A week after Alexander's homecoming, Joe decided to remove the bandage in the hope that the fresh air circulating around the wound would kick-start the healing. Nothing happened. The wound steadfastly refused to close.

Sixteen days after Alexander had come home I got a call at work on my mobile phone. It was Joe. He had been to examine Alexander again and he was now seriously concerned by the lack of improvement. He wanted to try something different. I was happy for him to do what he thought was best and whatever was necessary. I just wanted my horse to be fit again.

Joe's plan was to flush out the wound with a sterile liquid that he squeezed into the injury site out of special bags. He hoped this would remove anything buried deep down that might be causing infection and preventing recovery. His idea appeared to work. For a few days there were clear signs of improvement. The wound began to stop its endless seeping of gunk and healthy skin seemed to be developing. We allowed ourselves a small celebration.

Then the recovery process ground to a halt. The wound still stubbornly refused to close and resumed its leaking of yellow pus. Alexander was still not out of the woods. It was now more than six weeks since he had injured himself and he wasn't mending. Joe knew a veterinary surgeon called Peter Schofield, who worked at Hird & Partners equine hospital at Shelf, near Bradford, and he wanted him to take a look at Alexander. He was booked in for Monday, November 15.

We were on holiday that week and could take him ourselves but we weren't looking forward to the tow. It would take at least an hour and part of the journey involved negotiating narrow and winding rural roads with steep slopes, not ideal when pulling an injured horse.

The day could not have got off to a worse start. It was a freezing morning and the Land Rover refused to start. 'Mr Land Rover' always seemed to conk out at the worst possible moment. The Boss came to the rescue, driving to the village to give us a jump start.

We trundled to the yard, packed Alexander's things and led him to the trailer. As usual, he walked straight in but his rolling eye betrayed his anxiety. The only places we had towed him to were Skipton Horse Trials, for his saddle fitting, and Craven Country Ride. I'm sure that when he was loaded he still thought he was off to the races.

The Land Rover behaved impeccably on the journey but we breathed a sigh of relief as we pulled into the entrance yard at Shelf. Alexander was expected and several younger staff members seemed

Above: Alexander racing at Witton Castle (© Grossick Racing Photography).

Right: My first pony ride, aged four.

Below: An anxious Alexander on the day he arrived.

Above: Alexander after he suffered his serious injury.

Left: A confident Innes at her first competition (© Ruth Donnachie).

Below: Alexander's mother Gun Shot (left) leaps to victory at Southwell in July 2001 (photo courtesy of the Babbage family).

Above: Jenny (left), me and Sophie take the plunge with The Black Mare, Baby and Daniel at Craven Country Ride (© Matt Nuttall).

Below: Seconds from disaster ... jumping the 'house' at Somerford Park (© Joanna Prestwich).

Above: Jenny and the young Daniel in 2005.

Left: Going for it, on an early visit to Craven Country Ride (© Matt Nuttall).

Right: Flying the picket fence at Camp Hill (© Chris Lax Eventing).

Below: Ears pricked, Alexander easily takes me over a bigger fence (© Nick Gill).

Left: Showjumping at Eldwick (© Gresham Photography).

Above: Alexander rises to the occasion at an indoor event (© David Gaskell).

Below: Meeting Alexander's famous dad, Alflora, in November 2010.

Above: Competing in a one day event at Northallerton Equestrian Centre (© Paul Dobson).

Below: Worried looks from both of us at our first cross-country event.

Above: Another happy day at Camp Hill (© Richard Pickering).

Below: Figuring out a home-made 'skinny'.

Left: Sharing a quiet moment together.

Above: A view of the cross-country field in summer.

Below: Alexander grazing with his friends.

keen to see the new arrival. They looked out of the hospital door as he made an energetic entrance. He was lathered in sweat and bounced out of the trailer with me. His long neck strained to take in his new surroundings and he was unable to stand still as I held him on his lead rope. I was asked to walk him up and down and it was all I could do to hang on to him as he snorted and tugged at the rope.

The vets then asked me to take him into the examination room, where they could get to work. His injured leg was shaved and he was given an ultrasound test. It revealed that there was a foreign body in the leg. Our worst fears were realised. Alexander would have to have an operation under general anaesthetic. He was taken to the roomy stable where he would be staying and we prepared to say goodbye, or au revoir as we fervently hoped.

The operation would take place the next day. Any surgery on a horse, as with humans, carries a risk. There is always the possibility of a reaction to the anaesthetic. Like us, some horses react worse than others and can die. All we could do was go home and start worrying, and hope that we would see Alexander again.

Tuesday seemed to go on forever. We had been told the operation would take several hours and not to expect any news until the late afternoon. We tried to occupy ourselves at the livery yard but it was impossible to keep Alexander, and what was happening to him, out of our thoughts.

The afternoon dragged on. We placed Jenny's phone in front of us, willing it to ring. But it remained silent. The time crawled by. We had hoped to hear something, perhaps, by four o'clock. Four-thirty came and went. By 4.40pm, Jenny was starting to panic. The later it got the more convinced she was that Alexander was dead. At last, the phone rang. I looked at Jenny for some clue in her face. And then she simply said: 'Thank God,' and I knew Alexander was alive.

Veterinary surgeon Tim Booth had carried out keyhole surgery to get deep into the wound where debris had buried itself beyond the reach of our vet. He had removed a number of rotten tendon fragments and other bits of rubbish from the injury. No wonder it hadn't healed. Tim was confident the wound would now mend quickly. Alexander could be back in action in a matter of weeks. Then I would have the challenge of getting back on him.

Jenny had made a gloomy prediction when Alexander came into my life. Thoroughbreds are the Ferraris of the horse world but the delicacy of their turbo-charged make-up can mean they are more liable to break down. They have a reputation for always being injured. Back in May, Jenny had forecast: 'It will get broken, be on box rest for three months and you'll have to get back on it in the middle of winter.' Her prediction was looking spot on.

We visited Alexander the day after his operation. He was making very good progress and seemed happy in his stable, where he was clearly receiving five-star treatment. The standard of care and quality of surgery was to be more than repeated nearly two years' later when the life of another of our horses was at even greater risk.

Now we were looking forward to getting Alexander home. On the Friday, three days after his operation, we drove through dense fog to visit him and were given the all-clear.

It was exciting to turn up at the hospital with the trailer the next morning. Alexander, sporting yet another bright red bandage, marched up the ramp and the staff waved us off.

Back at the yard, I let my joy at having Alexander home get the better of me. After unloading him, I decided to manoeuvre the empty trailer round the back of the yard, between the muck heap and a pair of smart wooden stables built by a customer for his two horses. Passing the stables, I got my angles wrong and took off the edge of the roof with the top of the trailer. Jenny waved her arms and shouted at me to stop, but it was too late.

The Boss marched up and stood surveying the damage in silence, his roll-up fag smoking in the corner of his mouth. As he stared up at the roof, a piece of guttering detached itself and fell at his feet. It might have been a scene from Laurel and Hardy. Fortunately, the pair of horses were not in residence at the time. We learned later that The Boss had not only repaired the damage, but generously taken the blame, telling the stable owners he had done it himself.

Now Alexander was back, I could think about his recovery and about riding him again.

For the moment he remained confined to his box. But I soon saw signs of pink skin growing and the wound knitting together. He really was getting better. This time the recovery continued. As the days and weeks went by the improvement gathered pace. He would be left with scars, which would fade in time, but at last the injury was mending.

Alexander was a good patient. Occasionally, he would get frustrated at seeing his friends going out to the fields. But for the most part, he was relaxed and dealt with his confinement better than most horses.

The one notable exception was when someone led a Miniature Shetland pony past his box. It is odd that so many horses throw a panic attack when they encounter a tiny version of themselves. Alexander goggled in disbelief, his long orange neck straining to get a better view of the terrifying creature. He spun round in his red bandage and reared, getting both front legs caught up in his rug rack, and dangled helplessly as Jenny looked on in alarm. Enter Lorraine Coxon from the stable next door. She marched in, unhooked the thoroughbred and marched out again.

While Alexander was generally very easy to handle, I was preparing myself for an explosion when he did re-emerge from his stable.

In the week before Christmas, we got an early present from vet Joe. He was satisfied with the patient and discharged him. But now we were frustrated by the winter weather. Heavy snow had fallen on top of ice and we could not chance bringing Alexander out.

'We can't risk the bloody thing doing *Dancing On Ice* after all that time, effort and money,' said Jenny.

Four days after Christmas we were able to get Alexander on the horse walker. I watched, with thrill and trepidation, as he marched briskly round. It was good for him to be getting some exercise but frustrating for him to be confined. My nerves jangled more than once when he reared up mid-perambulation. But there was nothing I could do and he soon settled.

Back at work after the Christmas break, we had to rely on the seasonal goodwill of The Boss to lead Alexander on a rope, between his sessions on the walker. Alexander repaid him by leaping up and landing full weight on his foot.

The next recovery stage was to put Alexander in the lunging pen, a circular, high-sided enclosure where horses can be exercised loose or on a long rope. This gave him far more freedom and we expected him to let rip. Nervously, we shooed him into the pen, whipped off his headcollar and hastily retreated behind the metal gate, waiting for him to go crackers. But Alexander stood and blinked at us. He mooched around, sniffing at the sandy surface, stopped and blinked again. Baffled, we went in and tried to chase him round. He turned away, gave a small, half-hearted buck, cantered a few strides and stopped and blinked again. We returned him to his stable.

We got the explosive reaction we had been expecting the following day when he was turned out with Daniel in a small, grassy paddock. Alexander, with his little friend egging him on, charged around, throwing in huge bucks and twists. We feared he was going to leap out as he repeatedly ran at the fence before screeching to a halt. He was a terrifying sight and clearly feeling well.

On January 8, 2011, 102 days after he was injured, and in the depths of winter as Jenny had predicted, it was time for me to get on him again.

18

Keeping The Dream Alive

Alexander's injury was a devastating blow. But life with horses is a roller coaster of emotions, from exhilarating highs to terrible lows. The fact that they are large animals, bearing around half a ton of body weight, leaves them vulnerable to injuries that can plunge you into months of misery and anxiety. But you never know what unexpected highlight is just around the corner. And so it proved that winter.

Five days after Alexander was injured, and when he was still in hospital at Rathmell, we decided to cheer ourselves up by taking The Black Mare and Daniel indoor showjumping at Osbaldeston Riding Centre, near Preston. Osbaldeston has a long history in our family. It is where The Black Mare began jumping competitively more than a decade ago.

Teaching young horses to jump is a difficult and exacting process. You need patience, determination and courage. The Black Mare is now a jumping machine but when Jenny and Esme first took her to Osbaldeston it was the start of a depressing era of elimination and knock-downs and a hard lesson in the time it takes to achieve equestrian success.

'Clumsy cow,' Pat Fitton would groan sympathetically as the arena resounded to the clatter and thud of falling poles. Jenny was never sure if she meant horse or rider.

After yet another elimination at the yellow double, Jenny huddled under a horse blanket in the chilly viewing gallery as a glossy chestnut horse, with the snorting rubber-ball canter of the seasoned indoor showjumper, entered the ring. He had burgundy tasselled ear muffs and a matching velvet saddlecloth, emblazoned in gold piping with 'Mr Friskett'.

Mr Friskett clearly meant business. He did an equine version of rolling up his sleeves as he purposefully circled the ring, straining and frothing in his eagerness to power at the first jump. He scooted round the course, scarcely glancing at the fences, to earn a place in the long list of horses qualifying for the jump-off. To Jenny back then, the polished fluency of the likes of Mr Friskett seemed an unattainable aspiration.

Even though Osbaldeston is said to attract competitors from five counties, Esme and The Black Mare have notched up notable victories there, and Alexander and I would enjoy one of our finest earlier achievements in that arena.

Daniel had never been there before and we had no great expectations of him. He was by now a handy little showjumper, with a clutch of local prizes, but Osbaldeston, with its buzzing atmosphere and high number of quality competitors, was a very big ask.

My daughter Sophie had built a strong partnership with Daniel but she had never seen Osbaldeston before, let alone ridden there.

She had struggled with her nerves at events and this was going to be a big occasion for her. The Black Mare, however, was a seasoned campaigner and we had every reason to be confident she and Esme would do well.

The old indoor collecting ring at Osbaldeston could be challenging. It was tight for space, with little room for manoeuvre. There always seemed to be horses whizzing past your nose or back end, or leaping the two practice jumps. You needed a calm horse and your wits about you.

We arrived early to do the Clear Round class as a warm up before the competitive classes, and the collecting ring was still empty. I led Daniel round the edge to familiarise him with his new surroundings while Sophie got ready. He bounced around in a jaunty walk, tugging my arms out and snorting. It was like leading a racehorse round the parade ring before the start.

I should have known Dan well enough by now not to have been surprised. He always rose to the big occasion and he had been quick to recognise that this was an important place, somewhere to perform. It was like Coniston all over again. Sophie got on him. Although nervous, she was holding herself together well, focusing on the job in hand. When they entered the arena for their first clear round, Jenny and I dashed to the grandstand to watch.

Osbaldeston had not changed since Jenny and her daughter were regular visitors all those years ago. They were still playing the same Abba and Tom Jones songs. Now I was watching my daughter in the arena. The pair went round steadily and carefully and completed a successful clear round. A few minutes later, they came back and did the same again. Two out of two. And one proud dad.

Now it was the first class, 65cms in height, a bit more than the Clear Round class but well within Daniel's comfort zone. Sophie was starting to look very determined. I told her to take it steady and try to go clear to get into the jump-off. If the pair could manage that, they would have had a very successful day. There was plenty of quality opposition in the class, not least The Black Mare and Esme. There were 20 competitors and rosettes went to fourth, beyond Dan and Sophie's reach, I was sure.

Our horses survived the bustle of the collecting ring. The Black Mare was too experienced to bother about other horses. Daniel just wasn't bothered. The Black Mare was the first of our horses into the arena. There were no dramas as she jumped confidently clear.

Then it was Daniel's turn. I held my breath as he scuttled round, hopping from one fence to the next. Sophie steered a safe course, allowing him plenty of room to approach his fences. It worked. Daniel was clear. Both our horses were in the jump-off, with around a dozen others. The draw was made for the jump-off order. Daniel was the last to go.

'At least he'll know what he has to do to win,' I joked.

The Black Mare was among the first to jump. She flew round clear, a good three seconds faster than anything else. Several serious contenders threw down a challenge but none could get near her. And when there was only Daniel left to go, we realised she had won.

Now we were willing Sophie and Daniel to finish the day with another clear round. Jenny was eagerly anticipating one of the pretty pink rosettes that go to every competitor who jumps a double clear.

I went to see Sophie warming up in the collecting ring. 'Just try to go clear and enjoy it,' I said.

She and Daniel entered the arena and trotted slowly round. The bell went for them to start. The pair came into the first fence and hopped over it. As they landed, Sophie legged Daniel round the shortest route to the second jump. They cleared that safely and Sophie executed a motorbike turn into the next fence.

'My God. She's going for it,' I said.

Daniel is not the most stylish of horses but his scampering style covers the ground surprisingly quickly. And anyone who has ridden, and fallen off, him knows he can turn on a sixpence. Now Sophie was using that talent, spinning him round on the tightest of angles and kicking him into the fences. And Dan was jumping them. It was an extraordinary sight.

As the pair came into the second last fence, I glanced up at the big electronic clock ticking away their time. What I saw astonished me.

'Bloody 'ell, she could do this!' I exclaimed.

It was tight but it was possible. Sophie turned Dan one last time, on an impossible looking angle, into the final set of poles. She kicked, he jumped. The fence was still up and the pair surged through the finish. I looked up. The clock stopped. I had to think about the time. And then the commentator confirmed what was beginning to register in my head. They had won, pipping The Black Mare by an agonising three-tenths of a second.

Our horses were in first and second place. Unbelievably, Daniel was the victor. I could not have been prouder. For Sophie to go there for the first time and win was a remarkable achievement. To do it on Daniel was almost beyond belief.

Two weeks later, The Black Mare had her revenge, winning the same class. Daniel and Sophie finished a fantastic third. On our next visit, The Black Mare stepped up to the next class, at 75cms, and won again, beating no fewer than 44 rivals.

Osbaldeston was a happy diversion and I had another one during the long weeks and months Alexander was injured. Diane Blake, who kept a horse at the livery yard, approached me one day.

'Would you do me a favour?' she asked.

'Of course,' I replied, expecting a routine chore to help out. I couldn't have been further from the truth. Her next question stunned me.

'Would you mind taking Chester and galloping him up the cross-country field for me?'

I didn't have to think about that one. Chester was Diane's ex-racehorse. Like Alexander, he was chestnut with a white blaze, but there the resemblance ended. Chester, who had raced on the Flat and over hurdles under the name Amandari, was smaller and slighter. Now I owned Alexander I had developed a soft spot for chestnut thoroughbreds and Chester was a particular favourite of mine. He was gentle and sweet-natured and I always made sure I had a handful of treats when I passed his stable.

He was 14 years old. Diane had owned him for a couple of years after he retired from racing but she had suffered a nasty fall while galloping him across a field. Although not badly injured, she had lost confidence and was now only happy hacking him out down the lanes.

Diane said he needed to 'have a blast' now and again but he wasn't getting it. Knowing I had been doing just that with my own orange racehorse, she turned to me for help. I was delighted to accept and before you could say Red Rum, I was putting on my riding hat and boots while Diane tacked up Chester. I got on him and was immediately struck by how different he was from my own horse. He was noticeably smaller and I felt as if I was towering over him. He moved differently as well, taking a shorter stride. But he had that thoroughbred sway and bounce and I felt comfortable on him.

We walked down the lane, giving me time to get acquainted with him, and then Diane ushered us into the cross-country field. Chester began bouncing excitedly. It was a while since he had been in there. I kept a firm hold and spoke calmly to him and he obediently waited for my command. I could sense Diane watching, like an anxious mother, hoping her boy would behave and enjoy himself.

We began to trot. I could feel his desperation to go. But I didn't want it to be too soon. I needed to know I had control. As we came level with the steeplechase fence, I relaxed the reins and gave him a little squeeze with my lower leg. He didn't need to be asked twice. We charged up the hill, leaving Diane at the bottom. We were soon at the top and pulled up safely. Chester snorted and tossed his head with excitement. Diane came rushing up. She was laughing with delight.

'He loved that. Do you want to do it again?'

We galloped three times up the hill. Chester would have gone again if we had let him. It wasn't like galloping my own horse but it was great fun and it went some way towards making up for not being able to ride Alexander.

For the next couple of months, I rode Chester once or twice a week and loved every minute of it. We would gallop big circles in the bottom of the field, as well as running up it. After a while, Diane asked if I would jump him. Inevitably, I fell off.

I decided to start with a little log just inside the bottom gate. Not all racehorses, used to jumping big steeplechase fences or hurdles, take to other types of fences seen in cross-country and showjumping competitions. Being faced with something completely different, especially after a long racing career, can worry and confuse them. One ex-steeplechaser, who had twice completed the Grand National, refused to jump the first fence, a modest 2ft log, at a local hunter trial after his retirement.

Chester was used to jumping hurdles and he was very suspicious of the log. When we approached it for the first time, he took me by surprise by ducking out to the right. Feeling foolish in front of his owner, I gave him a crack with the whip, turned him into it again and rode with much more determination. Clearly worried, Chester ballooned the log and I went out the side door. Unlike Alexander, he did not gallop off without his rider. I was unscathed, except for embarrassment, and got back on with a leg up from Diane. The third time, Chester was more settled and we jumped the log together nicely. We did it again with a similar result and then picked off a couple more small fences, jumping them successfully. It had been a dramatic first jumping session. The first of several.

Chester was rushing into his fences as if he was still in a hurdle race. And he was more unpredictable and less confident than Alexander. He often did not see a stride to the fence. Sometimes, he got in too tight, sometimes he stood off a bit far: sometimes he dived at the fence, other times he gave it too much air. I found myself trying to guess how he would jump.

It was a test of my riding to build his confidence and to get him to jump more consistently. He was a quick learner and I soon persuaded him to approach his fences at a slower pace and to pay them more attention. He started to see a stride and suddenly we were popping over much more smoothly. I was chuffed and Diane would whoop with delight. But she was planning a new life in Canada and Chester was for sale. I would love to have bought him but there was no way I could afford another horse. He was sold to a young woman who moved him to a new home.

That autumn, Jenny and I went to meet Alexander's dad. I had contacted Peter Hockenhull, at the Shade Oak Stud in Shropshire where Alflora still lives, and is still siring, and he was happy for us to visit.

Alflora was born in 1989, raced on the Flat, winning five races, being placed 12 times, and earned more than £235,000. His grandfather was Nijinsky, one of the greatest racehorses ever. He is 16.3 hands and tends to sire big steeplechasers, like Alexander. Among his offspring is a chestnut chaser called Pearlysteps, who also has the same maternal grandfather, Gunner B, as Alexander, making him his closest relation currently racing under rules. Alflora is also the father of top chasers such as Wishfull Thinking, Wayward Prince and What A Friend.

Shade Oak is a large and influential stud farm and Peter Hockenhull was very busy when we arrived. But it did not prevent him from making time for us. At first he struggled to find Alflora. He wasn't in his field or stable. The stallion was tracked down to the steam room. My first sight of him left a lasting impression. Here was this tall, muscular dark bay horse, gleaming and steaming, and very proud of himself. It was the nearest I had ever been to a Derby runner and he looked every inch a star.

He was put on the indoor walker and marched round purposefully at a much faster speed than any horse at our yard. This was a real athlete. I often cajole Alexander when he slouches on our walker, telling him his dad is three times his age and can walk twice as fast!

Then came the highlight of the visit. Most stallions are sharp and lively and need special handling. I wasn't expecting to get too close to Alflora. But he is a very laid-back horse – a quality he seems to have passed down to Alexander – and after his handler had led him outside, I was offered his lead rope. And there I was, standing proudly at the head of Alexander's famous dad, holding him on the end of a rope. It was a 'Wow!' moment, captured by Jenny on a borrowed digital camera. We finished our grand day out with a super lunch at a local country pub, recommended by Peter.

I felt I had learned more about Alexander by meeting his dad. Some of Alflora's qualities, his gentle nature and laid-back attitude, for instance, I could see in Alexander. I hoped he had also inherited his dad's 'Never say die' spirit. I mused about the horse I now owned. I had not realised when I got him that he was so fresh off the racecourse. It would have made no difference to my decision to have him. But it did explain his liveliness.

I thought too about how strange fate can be. The favourite in Alexander's last race at Dalston was also pulled up. But Hunt Ball has since taken a very different course in life.

He too was sold but he went into a professional racing yard and in the 2011-12 season he was the most improved jumps horse in training, winning seven races, including one at the Cheltenham Festival. He also got third place in a Grade 1 race at the Aintree Grand National meeting, when he had behind him Sir Alex Ferguson's Cheltenham Gold Cup horse, What A Friend – a son of Alflora. Following Hunt Ball round clearly runs in the family!

Hunt Ball was being aimed at the 2013 Cheltenham Gold Cup, but instead went for another race at the Festival. The following year he finished fourth in the Ryanair Chase at Cheltenham.

My Alexander didn't get another chance at racing. But I am so glad he didn't, or he would never have been 'my Alexander'. I am sure Hunt Ball has a wonderful life but I would bet he is no happier than his former race rival, Adelphi Warrior. I have a collection of ten wonderful racing photos of Alexander that I found on professional photographer John Grossick's website. Two of them show him jumping a fence ahead of Hunt Ball – a real claim to fame.

None of this knowledge was going to make it any easier for me to get back on my own racehorse after he had been on box rest for three months. I was about to find out if I could cope.

19

Accidents Will Happen

While the sight of Alexander bucking round the small paddock was disconcerting, it must have got rid of some of his pent-up frustration. And so getting back on him was not as dramatic as I feared. I stood on the mounting block, slung my right leg over his back and went with him as he started walking unasked.

He certainly had a spring in his step but he didn't seem ready to kill me just yet. He walked purposefully out of the yard, but there were no huge bucks or any sign of a mad wobbly that might send a family of ramblers scattering for cover. We marched off down the lane and I was so glad to be riding him again that my worries disappeared. I didn't want to push my luck the first time so we just walked a few hundred yards, with Jenny anxiously trying to keep pace. Alexander seemed pleased to be out and about again and, as we turned for home, he started jogging enthusiastically.

Jogging is not to be encouraged, the horse should either walk or trot at the rider's command, not go at a pace in between when he fancies. Alexander was meant to be walking but I was having such fun I didn't care, so we jogged back to the stables.

On the next ride, we ventured further. We passed the bottom of the cross-country field without any tantrums and trotted up the steeply sloping lane beyond it, where I planned to turn round. But Alexander had other ideas. Clearly wanting to go on, he refused to return down the hill and started to rear. Then he reversed on two legs towards a ditch, a reminder of the cunning protest tactic he had used with Ian and Karen Conroy. Jenny, who was riding Daniel, was dismayed. A group of up to 15 hikers was striding merrily up the lane towards us, oblivious of the danger.

Daniel stood quietly, watching the drama unfold. He seemed to be saying to Alexander: 'What's yer problem, mate?' I managed to keep my balance, stay in the saddle and make Alexander move forward and head down the hill. We got back without any more alarms, although Alexander frothed and jogged 20 yards ahead of Daniel all the way.

For the next couple of weeks, Alexander used the rear and reverse ploy at the same place. On one occasion he did it as a family of walkers approached. Their fearful expressions made it clear they wished they had taken another route.

Another favourite spot for Alexander's backward manoeuvres was further along the lane, at a cluster of holiday homes that used to be the Fitton family's racehorse training stables, stud farm and riding school. I dealt with each episode by relaxing my hands and shoving him forward with my lower leg. Soon, he began to settle into more normal behaviour and our hacks out became less challenging.

In February, I took him into the outdoor arena for some serious flatwork training. Alexander had done little or no schooling. Although he has naturally good paces and movement and is a quick learner, he was not at all keen. Schooling is hard work for both horse and rider. It is akin to physical training for a human athlete. You have to push your horse to make him use his body and bend himself in the right way to become fit and flexible. It is the essential groundwork for all riding, including the jumping side.

But Alexander hated it. The longer he was in the school and the more I asked him to do, the more frustrated he became. Ten minutes was about his limit before he began to protest. This took the form of going backwards, or going up, and would be signalled by an angry tossing of the head and shaking of the body. Jenny, watching from outside the school, could see it coming from the wild rolling of his eye.

I was getting invaluable schooling help from Sue Chapman, a good friend on the yard who we have known for years. When Esme and The Black Mare won the Pre-Novice class at Coniston Hunter Trials in 2006 – beating Sue by just one second – it was our friend who paid for the champagne celebrations.

Sue evented her horse Star to a good standard and she is always ready to assist others with their inexperienced or troublesome horses. She is a rider I really look up to and I value her advice and guidance more than most.

The first thing she taught me was to ignore Alexander's tantrums in the school and to carry on with the work as if nothing had happened. The worst thing to do was to have an argument with him. I quickly learned to discipline Alexander in such a way that he did not realise he was being disciplined: to sit the rearing and to push him firmly forward. Before he knew what was happening, he was trotting, bending, or circling, and had forgotten what he was objecting about. The key was to keep him busy, keep his mind occupied and not to use the whip. He reacted like a spoiled child to the whip. An angry look came into his eyes and he bucked and shook himself violently in protest.

When I first began riding him down the lane, he leapt forward if I raised my whip hand to acknowledge a motorist who had slowed down for us. He obviously thought it was a signal to go faster, still fresh in his head after racing. He is so laid-back now I sometimes have to wave a whip at him to encourage better effort. Very occasionally, I have to give him a little tap on the shoulder with it to focus his mind. He throws me a hurt look and then gets on with the job, though he still springs forward. The racing memories are still there. Usually, I don't bother carrying a whip. With a horse like Alexander, it is largely redundant, which suits me fine.

Sue was pleased with our flatwork but made me work harder on my circles, saying I rode 'very good triangles'! The truth is that, although I tried hard in my lessons, I wasn't that much keener on schoolwork than Alexander: all either of us really wanted to do was gallop and jump. I did better during a lesson in the showjumping field when Sue had us executing technical bounces and grid work. She also helped me by riding Alexander herself when I was at work. She reported the odd rodeo session but was delighted with how he had improved.

Two months after getting back on, I was galloping Alexander up the cross-country field again. Ladies at the Yard said I was brave after we took a flying leap over the Loch Ness Monster fence, so named because it is built from upturned half-tyres of different sizes. I aimed him at the smaller tyres but, in his exuberance, he towed me over the biggest part of the jump and bucked with excitement on landing.

Our first outing after Alexander's injury was to Craven Country Ride for the Easter Trail Ride. The day was a huge success. We jumped well together and I stuck on when he jinked as he put in a big leap at another spruce fence. Everything was going well and my confidence was growing. But then things began to unravel.

On May 1, Jenny and I went to the annual point-to-point race meeting at Heslaker near Skipton, held at the same venue as Skipton Horse Trials. We enjoyed our day out, though it was marred by the death of a horse that collapsed from a heart attack in the first race. Joe McKinder was one of the duty vets and he was with the horse in seconds. He said it was probably dead before it hit the ground.

One horse running was a seven-year-old chestnut mare called Fresh Fruit, who was sired by Alflora. In the racing world, horses with the same father are not classed as brothers and sisters. That is only the case when they have the same mother. But in my eyes, completely smitten as I am by my own racehorse, any son or daughter of Alflora is a blood relative and I regard them as a half-brother or half-sister of Alexander. So I avidly follow the fortunes of steeplechasing stars such as What A Friend, Wishfull Thinking, Wayward Prince, Alfie Spinner and Alasi – all sired by Alflora. Over the years, I have lost a fair amount of money on 'the brothers', having gambled on them and then tuned into *Channel 4 Racing* to watch them fall over or trail in out of the money.

That day at Skipton Races I was in the money for once as I cheered Fresh Fruit to the easiest win of the day. She was so far ahead on the final circuit of the track that her jockey was able to slow her to a canter at one point.

I had wondered whether Alexander should have another spin at racing. After all, he hadn't been given a real chance to shine and he was clearly an athlete. I even thought about having him trained so I could ride him in a race. To be able to jump round a course on such a wonderful horse and pit my wits against other jockeys seemed a dream made in heaven. After all, my grandad had done it – why not me?

I thought about how I would ride Alexander in a race. I felt he was more of a stamina horse than a speed horse, with a safe, springy jump, like most Alflora offspring. I would keep him handy in about third or fourth place and hold him up until after the final fence, trying to keep something in reserve, and then ride out to the line. One race would be enough and in my head I won it every time.

With that dream in mind, I strode out to the final fence at Skipton to have a good look at it before the racing began.

First I checked the landing side. I stood next to the fence. It came up to my chest and it looked very solid. But there was no drop and I felt it wouldn't be beyond me. Then I walked round to the take-off side and my bravado deserted me. The fence was the same heady height but it sloped a good three feet towards me. You would have to take off at least a further yard back from that, so you would be flying – several feet in the air – for yards. All at a full gallop. And this fence didn't have a ditch in front of it as some of them do.

The enormity of the task and the immense bravery needed to take it on dawned on me and reality suddenly kicked in. This was just a dream. Hats off to grandad. He had more courage than me.

Nor could I risk Alexander. Although steeplechasing is a wonderful spectacle, and everything is done these days to safeguard the horses, there are still casualties. What would be the amazing sight of Alexander in full flight again was far outweighed by the potential, however small, of harm befalling him. He was not a racehorse any more. He was my big orange pet.

The next day I came down to earth with a hell of a bump. I rode Alexander, with Jenny on Daniel, and we ventured into the cross-country field. I decided to jump a new fence The Boss had constructed at the bottom of the meadow. It is a line of three old telegraph poles of different heights and widths. We skipped safely over the first small pole and then lined up for the middle, medium-sized obstacle. Alexander jumped it effortlessly but as he landed he shot off to the right and began to turn himself inside out. Before I even knew I had a problem, I slammed into the hard ground with my left knee. Stunned and in pain, I stayed down as Alexander hurtled away up the field.

Jenny said later that he had twisted so high in the air, with all four legs off the ground, that all she could see was the underneath of his ginger tummy. As I lay prone she feared I was really seriously hurt. She did not know whether to come to my aid or try to catch Alexander and then go for help. She went for the second option after I told her my knee hurt but I was all right. I wasn't convinced and I lay there for a full five minutes until the pain began to subside.

When I did move, the best I could manage was to spin sideways on the ground. My knee seemed to be bending, which was good news. But it had already swelled up to twice its normal size and there was a hole in my jodhpurs through which protruded bloody flesh. I feared I might have broken or cracked the kneecap.

Carefully, I sat up and then, with an effort, got to my feet. The knee was still throbbing but I could put weight on it. It seemed I had been fortunate. I was on my own. As I stood there it seemed an awful long way to the top of the hill, and I certainly wouldn't be marching up it. I set off at a steady hobble and was relieved to be able to do so. Moving the knee obviously helped and the further I limped the freer it got. But I was still in considerable pain.

I must have gone at a reasonable speed because I had reached the top of the field, limped down Muddy Lane and was just 300 yards from the stables when Jenny appeared, riding pillion alongside The Boss as he raced to the rescue in his big yellow digging machine. Fearing what they might find, she was amazed to see me hobbling along.

'I thought you were dead,' she said.

I asked anxiously after Alexander. I was afraid that his flight had taken him riderless on to the lane, where he could have met traffic. But he had stopped at the top of the field and Jenny was able to catch him and lead him safely back to the yard. I was relieved but Jenny was less concerned. Her fear for me had turned to anger about what Alexander had done.

When I considered why it had happened, a number of contributory reasons emerged. The first explanation was that Alexander had simply got over-excited about jumping something new and his head had uncontrollably exploded. This was not good, but there were also mitigating factors. A few yards beyond the fence a bog had developed following heavy rain. Alexander might have landed at the edge and veered away from it, which would explain his sharp right turn.

He also had a loose sarcoid on his left flank, beneath his tail. Sarcoids are like unsightly warts. They are quite common in younger horses and have to be treated because they can turn cancerous. Alexander had three large sarcoids when we bought him. Our vet had treated them with a special cream that slowly burns and shrivels them away until they drop off. One of Alexander's had already gone, another on his side showed no signs of disappearing yet, but the one under his tail seemed nearly ready to go and may have caused him some discomfort when he jumped.

I felt it was wrong to point the finger of blame too firmly at the horse. Jenny, who had had a bad scare, was less sympathetic. 'It can go back to racing,' she said.

When the Ladies at the Yard saw me limping about in my ripped, bloodied and grass-stained jodhpurs they urged me to go to hospital for a check-up. But I knew that, though badly bumped, bruised and scraped, the knee was not seriously injured.

What I needed was a drink. The jodhpurs were in danger of sticking to the wound so I cut the knee out of them and dragged myself up to the pub for a lager and a roast beef Sunday lunch. Diners at The Cross Keys turned in consternation as I hobbled to a sunny, outdoor table overlooking the canal and pastureland. I was doing nothing to banish the fears of many parents with pony-mad offspring that horse riding is a highly dangerous sport!

I was out of action for two weeks and then got back on for a leisurely walk and trot down the lane. Meanwhile, Sue took Alexander for a long ride out through the spring countryside and the loose sarcoid flew off when they had a vigorous uphill gallop.

The fall had taught us some lessons about handling and managing Alexander. He was our first thoroughbred and we were learning the hard way that they have to be dealt with differently. Our mistakes had contributed to the fall. We should have taken him for a long hack out before jumping a new fence. We should have checked the ground first. And we should have thought twice about jumping him at all with a loose sarcoid. We would have to be more careful in future.

I had learned a painful lesson. Alexander was not a pet. He was an athlete and I had to treat him as such. He was certainly not Jenny's cup of tea but she was about to meet the horse of her dreams.

20

Good Times Bad Times

The fall from Alexander came a week after the death of our beloved lurcher Denny, fondly known as Mrs Dog. Approaching her 14th birthday, she had slowed down a bit but she still loved her walks on the village green, wading across the river when it was low or skipping over the stepping stones.

On Easter Sunday, we were returning from our morning river walk when she collapsed from some sort of catastrophic seizure. I carried her home in my arms and laid her on her favourite doggy cushion in the kitchen. We summoned the vet but there was nothing that could be done and Mrs Dog was put to sleep. She slipped away quickly and peacefully on her cushion with her family around her.

We were heartbroken. She is still terribly missed and the flowered urn containing her ashes remains on the shelf in the tack room at home. Her lead, collar and coat hang untouched behind the pantry door.

Denny was an integral part of our family. She was the gentlest of dogs and liked nothing better than to curl up in the gentleman's chair, which was meant for me, in front of the log burning stove in the living room, with her chin resting on the arm and her big, brown eyes gazing at us. That is something that can never be replaced, but in time I hope we will be able to laugh about the many happy times we had with her, rather than mourn her.

Sadly, the loss of Denny was just the start of nine months of personal tragedies Jenny and I were to suffer. The next death was that of George the ferret. While he might 'only' have been a little furry creature, he was again part of the family and gave us all hours of fun.

When I met Jenny, she cared for more than a dozen rescue ferrets. Most of them lived in a big pen at the back of the cottage but the spare room upstairs was home to some.

When Jenny began working full-time at the *Telegraph & Argus*, their numbers dwindled as they died and were not replaced. The spare room became part of the house again. In time, the outside pen was ripped down and a large hutch took its place for the remaining ferrets. Eventually, only George was left.

George was everybody's favourite, a real livewire who loved playing and would scuttle backwards on two legs ridiculously, race madly around the kitchen and clamber up and down my back and lick my head. He was a bundle of energy and it was awful to see his back end go, signalling the end. I didn't think I could cry for a ferret, but saying goodbye to George, and to albino ferret Raffles, who died before him, was a tearful experience.

In the late summer, Jenny learned that her brother, Martin, who lived in France with his wife, had a brain tumour. The news came totally out of the blue. Martin lived a healthy life, growing organic food at his idyllic converted barn home and he seemed to have everything going for him. He had an operation to remove the tumour. It went well but the brain tumour was secondary to lung cancer. Three months after the initial diagnosis, he lost his fight for life. He was only 52.

It was, of course, a terrible shock for Jenny and all her family. She had managed to speak to Martin by phone during his illness, but regretted not travelling to France to see him. We had hoped he would recover enough to be able to visit us and the horses – he was an accomplished rider as a young man – but it was not to be.

In the space of just a few days, early in 2012, I lost three relatives. My aunt and uncle, Doreen and Gordon, both died. Aunty Doreen was in her late eighties and lived in a nursing home near York. Uncle Gordon, who was 90, emigrated to Canada when I was very young. He was still living at home with his wife when he got terminal cancer.

Around the same time, we also lost my young cousin, Michael, who died in sudden and tragic circumstances. At his inquest, the coroner recorded a verdict of misadventure and Michael's death remains a terrible mystery. He was just 31. He had recently been promoted at work and everything was going well for him. He was popular, and a wonderfully caring person with a terrific sense of humour, who was a tower of strength to his family. In particular, he was a rock, ally and true friend to his mum and dad, Jenny and Mike. I owe him a personal debt of gratitude. Michael was always mature beyond his years and I will never forget his kindness to me and sensible advice when my marriage was in difficulties.

In September 2011, Esme, then aged 22, left home to start a career in Bristol, taking The Black Mare with her. Jenny was philosophical about them going but I knew it was a big loss for her. With the death of Denny, the three ladies with her at the start of her new life in the Yorkshire Dales nine years earlier – Esme, The Black Mare and Mrs Dog – would all be gone.

It was a poignant moment to hug her daughter and wave the pair of them off as they set out from the livery yard in a huge horse wagon containing all their possessions, The Black Mare peering anxiously through a small, barred window in the back. It was a big change for Jenny but another black horse had already come into our lives.

On May 21, the first anniversary of Alexander's dramatic arrival, and less than a week after I had begun riding him again after my fall, we went to Grange-over-Sands to meet Ian and Karen Conroy for the first time. The purpose of our visit was for me to find out more about Alexander's background. We took along professional photos of him paddling in the water complex at Craven Country Ride and Ian and Karen were pleased with how well and happy 'Herman' looked.

After chatting and looking round the yard where Alexander had lived, we all took a stroll up the fields, high above the spectacular estuary, to see the couple's young horses. They were a contented and handsome looking bunch, real quality animals that anyone would want to buy. More than one caught our eye, including a small, stocky, jet black mare who was very busy and keen to push her way to the front and be noticed. 'There's me!' she seemed to be saying.

We lingered around these wonderful horses until it was time to return down the fields. I had been deep in conversation with Ian, finding out as much as I could about Alexander, and hadn't really studied the individual horses. But as we walked back something suddenly struck Jenny, and she returned to look again at the little black mare who had been seeking our attention. And then it hit her.

'She's just like our black mare. They're almost identical. She's just a younger version,' she said. The likeness was indeed remarkable.

Jenny asked Karen about her. She was an Irish-cross thoroughbred, just like our mare, and not yet three years old. Her mother, who was also at the stud farm, was a retired racehorse called Goldengirlmichelle who had won three hurdle races. Her dad was the famous event stallion Jumbo, whose offspring included Badminton Horse Trials winner Headley Britannia. Consequently, Ian and Karen had nicknamed her Nellie.

We could not afford another horse and it would be totally irresponsible to buy one, but over the next few days Jenny could not get Nellie out of her head. Her favourite horse, The Black Mare, was leaving for a new life. She had lost, or was losing, some of the most precious people and animals she had. Here, perhaps, was a little horse who could give her fresh hope and purpose.

'She's my perfect horse, Steve,' she said.

Nellie was for sale. Ian and Karen, having seen how Alexander had thrived under our care, were keen that we should have the first option of buying her and had offered her to us at a very reasonable price. But we would have to get on with it if we were going to buy her. It would not be fair to keep Ian and Karen waiting when they could quite easily sell her elsewhere.

The only way we could think about buying Nellie was to put one of our horses on part loan. It would have to be Daniel because we could not risk anyone else riding Alexander.

We placed adverts in our local papers and farm shops and by June we had found a lady who would pay us to ride Daniel two or three times a week. That allowed us to consider the purchase of Nellie. It would not be easy paying for the upkeep of three horses, but with the part loan we would just be able to do it.

Now Jenny had to find the money to buy her. Her dad, Alan, helped with that. Knowing money was always tight he made a generous contribution. He had been expecting Jenny to get another dog, rather than a horse, but the heartbreak of losing Denny was still too raw.

Jenny made two more visits to Cumbria to see the little black mare and each time was more convinced that she was just the horse for her. And so, on August 6, a week before Jenny's 54th birthday, Nellie arrived in a trailer with Ian and Karen. A violent storm flared, with thunder and lightning, just as they were expected. But it blew over and the sun came out to welcome them.

A little black bundle of energy came bounding out of the trailer and tugged Ian off towards the canal bridge. We put Nellie with The Black Mare in a tiny paddock behind the café. The pair seemed happy with each other but they looked so similar we were struggling to tell who was who.

We watched anxiously as the new arrival explored her little field. She did not seem fazed by her new surroundings and had that same energy and purpose we had noticed the first time we saw her. Then she started to make threatening moves towards the fence. Knowing that she had jumped out over a fence in Cumbria we worried that she might repeat the trick so we decided to let her go out in the big meadow alongside the canal with all the other mares. It was a risk because she would have to be accepted by the herd and if she got too pushy she could get kicked. But anything was a risk at this stage and it seemed better than her going over the fence and getting loose on the lane.

Worried sick, we watched her in the meadow for more than an hour. Although she was keen for someone to befriend her, she was sensible about it and kept a safe distance. We noticed that a couple of the older mares were protecting her and we hoped all would be well. Reluctantly, we tore ourselves away.

Early the next morning, Jenny rang the yard to make sure she was safe, and she was. She would stay out in the field, getting used to her new surroundings, for a few weeks before taking The Black Mare's stable when she left.

Nellie was soon accepted by the other mares and became firm friends with an ex-racehorse called Cinders. The pair were often to be found lying down close together on the warm summer mornings. Like me with Alexander, Jenny wanted to give Nellie a name of her own. Because she was small, black and Irish, we called her Innes – half of Guinness.

After more than a year together, and fully recovered from my tumble, Alexander and I at last began competing. I targeted a one-day event at Richmond Equestrian Centre in North Yorkshire for our first outing. It involved a simple walk and trot dressage test, showjumping and a rustic working-hunter course. The jumping phases would be over 2ft fences, less than half the height Alexander had been used to when racing, but a big enough challenge for us as a partnership.

We practised hard for our big day. Alexander was still unenthusiastic about schooling but he was starting to accept that it had to be done. The same could be said for me. Although the cross-country phase was the exciting bit, no matter how good our jumping was we wouldn't have a chance of any prizes if our dressage test was poor.

David Elms gave me a showjumping lesson and had us doing technical grids and bounces into fences before tackling a course of jumps. Racehorses can find showjumping difficult, because of the different technique, but Alexander seemed to have a natural talent for it. He always set off in the slow, rhythmic, bouncy canter needed, and jumped mostly out of stride.

Some horses are unnerved by brightly coloured showjumps, or garishly designed fillers, placed underneath the poles as an added difficulty. But Alexander was untroubled. Whatever the fence, he came bouncing in and sprang over it without a second glance, and then looked for the next one.

His enthusiasm was helping me. I had always considered myself better suited to cross-country riding, where bravery counts more than style, and I had felt too short of technique to be a successful showjumper. But now I had a horse that was taking me round without me having to kick and I was able to relax more. With David's help, I was sitting up in the saddle and staying still. My back was now straight, my shoulders back, my head up: I was looking beyond the fence, instead of down at the ground, and I was going with the horse as he jumped.

David was particularly impressed with how we tackled the grids and bounces, describing them as 'fab'. He was less pleased with one or two of my tight turns into fences, making it much more difficult for a big horse like Alexander to get into his stride. They were 'pants'.

We went to Richmond with David and his wife Joanne, who was competing on her strapping part-Shire horse, Father Ted. The two horses travelled well together but Alexander had sweated up and was excitable when we got there. His long neck craned out of the side door of the trailer and his eyes rolled. But his behaviour was near perfect as we tacked him up and I got on him.

As I sat astride my edgy thoroughbred, I felt nervous but I was looking forward to the day. This was what I had dreamed of and had been working towards. I was about to find out what it felt like to compete on a real quality athlete. Alexander looked impressive with his plaited mane and leggy muscular frame. I was wearing my smart black showjumping jacket, gold fox's head stock pin and white dressage gloves. I really felt the part.

The dressage was indoors and we pranced from the wagon park to the warm-up arena. It was big, which was a bonus. The more room we had for manoeuvre, the better. There were only a couple of horse and rider combinations warming up when we entered the collecting ring but it was enough to make Alexander twitchy. He felt like a coiled spring as we walked and trotted round and I concentrated on keeping the lid on him by relaxing my hands, moving him forward and talking quietly to him. He tugged his head around but I had control.

All too soon it was time to enter the main arena. The dressage was the part I was least looking forward to. It was only the second test I had ever ridden. The first was some years ago when Daniel and I took part in a combined dressage and working-hunter competition. At that stage, my riding was rough and ready and Daniel was not inclined to help much. There were only three competitors in the class and I was amazed to discover that we were leading after the dressage, despite the fact that I couldn't get Daniel to canter. Then I found out that our two rivals had withdrawn. With four faults in the jumping phase, I was proud to receive a first-place rosette, even if it was by default.

Now Alexander and I were facing our dressage debut, and even though the test was as simple as they come, I was worried I would not remember it, or that we would make a mess of it. But for a first attempt it went surprisingly well. There were no mistakes and I was delighted with our mark of 57.82 per cent – equivalent to a score of just over 42. Any score below 40 is reasonable, so we weren't far off.

The judge's comments were: 'A very nice horse with good paces, just a little tense today. Calmly ridden.' In addition, Alexander's behaviour in the arena was impeccable, which boded well for the future.

Our showjumping round drew praise from the watching David. Alexander went into his wonderful bouncy canter and jumped everything. We would have had a clear round had I not lost my way after the first fence and been forced to circle, costing us four faults and some stern criticism from Jenny, captured on Sophie's mobile phone recording of the round.

Sophie and Jenny's blunt, unscheduled commentaries would become an amusing backdrop to our performances over the coming months. Jenny is herself very adept at taking the wrong course. She lost out on a top place at a local riding club show by missing out fence three in a four-fence jump-off.

Alexander was equally keen in the working-hunter phase, towing me into the fences but carelessly knocking a couple of poles off with his front legs. We ended with 12 jumping penalties to add to our dressage score. Happy with our day, I loaded Alexander into the trailer ready to go home.

We had finished some minutes before Joanne and Ted, who were still jumping round the working-hunter course. Without his friend, Alexander's insecurity kicked in. He strained his neck to try to catch sight of him, without success, and then started to panic. He was sweating and as I tried to calm him he began frantically weaving his head from side to side, a wild look in his eyes. He was swaying with such energy the trailer was starting to rock. At the same time, he was letting out huge, shuddering neighs.

It seemed as if he was going to erupt, but slowly, as I stood stroking his neck and quietly reassuring him, he began to settle, and when Ted hove into sight peace was restored. But it would take some time yet for Alexander to put his worries and anxieties aside.

Our efforts had earned us a bright yellow third-place rosette. There were actually only three competitors in the class but the scores were close and we had only lost out through a slightly inferior dressage test. I was thrilled that we had been competitive and felt we had something to build on.

Next on the agenda was a bigger one-day event at a different venue in North Yorkshire. It would include cantering in the dressage and a much tougher cross-country challenge. When Jenny and I walked the course the day before the event, we agreed it was asking too many questions of us. Solid wooden rails and big drops were difficult enough, but add to that the technical nature of the course and it was too soon.

Instead, we went to Northallerton Equestrian Centre for the first time, though it would not be the last. We love it there. The organisers are friendly and helpful, the facilities are first class and the courses are challenging but fair.

I had entered a one-day event, again at 2ft high and with the same dressage test. The showjumping was indoors. It was a small arena for a big horse like Alexander and we had one fence down. The dressage was outdoors this time. I don't know if that played a part but Alexander was excitable, cutting his corners and generally being 'onward bound'. It is not what you want for the controlled discipline of dressage. Our score was 45.65, worse than at Richmond, though the judge described Alexander as 'a beautiful horse'. But it put us out of the running for a rosette.

Our cross-country round was clear, but not without drama. The course was contained in one field and the fences were mainly straightforward rustic poles. Alexander was keen as mustard and I had to take a big pull on the reins after he launched himself over the first obstacle. But, encouragingly, he was listening to me. When I asked him to steady up, he did, and in return I let him tow me over the jumps. He leaped exuberantly round the first half of the course and we were cantering towards a corner of the field before turning to face the next fence when, without warning, he reared up and spun away to the right.

I was taken completely by surprise but managed to stay in the saddle and, as he came back down to earth, I tried to make him walk forward but he went straight up in the air and veered off again. Once more I stuck tight and this time he moved on reluctantly. We made the turn and he then carried on as if nothing had happened. We finished by flying on and off the Devil's Dyke, a bank between a line of bushes. Jenny was certain we would be penalised, or even eliminated, for the rearing fit but because we weren't presenting at a fence, it didn't cost us anything.

So why had Alexander behaved in this way? We decided that the sight of a big white mobile commentary box in the corner of the field where he was heading was an unpleasant reminder of his racing days and was the cause.

We were delayed leaving the event by a flat tyre on the Land Rover. I am not the most practical man around. My flawed way of tying up a haynet means the knot gets so tight Jenny has to cut it down the next morning. 'Can someone put it up for me?' is a familiar cry to the Ladies when I am alone at the yard, with a haynet over my shoulder.

So changing a tyre gave us a headache. I spent what seemed an age messing about underneath the Land Rover, trying to find where the jack should attach to. The more I fiddled, the more annoyed Jenny got and the more we began to fall out. Just when we thought we would be terminally stuck on the showground, the day was saved by a kind-hearted chap from a nearby trailer. He was used to similar vehicles and sorted it for us in no time at all. But our predicament had made home seem a long way off and we were very relieved to pull up safely at the yard two hours later.

Alexander displayed so much energy the next morning that we decided to take him to his first showjumping event, at Eldwick Show, just along the moor road from Sue and Harvey Smith's racing stables.

Northallerton had not taken much out of him because I was subjected to more rearing fits. The first came in the collecting ring when a tiny pony went trotting past in an adjoining warm-up field. As we waited to enter the showjumping arena, more small ponies came by. Alexander watched them in horror. We were reminded of the time he was on box rest and panicked when a Miniature Shetland Pony was walked past his stable. He alternately ran for cover to the back of his box and dashed to the front to see if the terrifying apparition was still there. Clearly, he had a tiny pony phobia.

Once in the arena he settled into a nice rhythm. We had two goes at the non-competitive Clear Round class, having one fence down, and I decided to enter the 2ft 6ins class. This was a bigger height than our previous showjumping efforts but I was confident. My faith was justified as Alexander jumped fluently and, with one fence to go, we were still clear and heading for the jump-off.

Then he spotted the ponies. In the next field, a showing class had been taking place and the rosettes were about to be handed out. As we jumped the second-last fence, a line of small ponies appeared in our eyeline. Alexander panicked and reared. My feet shot out of the stirrups as Alexander went vertical but I managed to steer him in the direction of the final obstacle, a set of solid-looking planks, and booted him stirrupless into it. But Alexander was still panic-stricken and, with his head stuck up in the air, he charged through the top plank without looking.

That was the end of my jump-off hopes. To rub salt into my wounds, I was told off by an official for leaving the arena with my feet out of the stirrups. Jenny had a good laugh at my ridiculous antics but it had been another positive day. Alexander had jumped confidently and we were very much going in the right direction.

My focus was now on Somerford Park. In just over five weeks, I would be taking Alexander there for the first time. But first there was an intriguing interlude that put our horses in the national spotlight.

21

Picture This

The call came out of the blue. Horses were needed to be part of a work of art by well-known social photographer Red Saunders for an exhibition at the Impressions Gallery in Bradford. He was creating a living tableau of an English Civil War scene and he wanted a couple of horses to be in it. It meant us travelling at the weekend to a remote location in Bronte Country for the photographic session. It had its challenges but it sounded like an entertaining day out. Anyway, the fact that we were being paid £200 convinced us it was worth doing. As Jenny said: 'It pays the electricity bill.'

We checked out the route and it was straightforward until we got through Keighley. After that, we were towing two horses up into the unknown along hilly rural roads. Jenny drove, as I had not yet learned to tow the horse trailer. Once we had climbed out of Keighley and reached the moors we began to realise the awkwardness of the task. The lane narrowed so that in many places it wasn't wide enough for two vehicles to pass. It wound through tiny hamlets and plunged up and down frighteningly steep hills. In strange and demanding territory, Jenny became increasingly worried.

At last we passed a remote reservoir and reached our turn-off. This presented a difficulty of its own. The left turn was at a right angle to the lane. The track we were turning into was even narrower and went over a stone bridge before bending immediately sharp right into a steep, uphill climb, surrounded by high grassy banks and grazing sheep. It took ten minutes of anxious manoeuvring to get us going up the incline. With enormous relief we reached the top and parked in a large field in front of the farmhouse that was being used as a control centre for the photo shoot.

The views were breathtaking, sweeping miles over the valley to further hills and isolated farmsteads. In the distance tiny horses, cattle and sheep cropped the upland pasture, like plastic miniatures on a model railway board. The sun beat down, turning the spectacular scenery into a shimmering mirage.

More than 40 local people, dressed in period costume, were involved in the photo shoot. Alexander was to be the horse of the captain of the soldiers. Originally, an 'extra' in full regalia was lined up to sit on him but we were extremely worried about that arrangement. It was to be someone who couldn't ride, let alone handle an unpredictable thoroughbred. What if Alexander was spooked by the costume and tried to run off with his rider?

The organisers saw the sense of what we were saying and asked me to take the captain's part. I was ushered into the temporary costume and make-up room to be transformed into a Cromwellian cavalry officer. I emerged in thigh-high leather boots and spurs, metal gauntlets over my hands and a feathered hat, much to Jenny's amusement. Sophie was invited to feature as a soldier. The pair of us looked quizzically at each other, with a sense of being part of a strange fantasy world.

The next step was to get on Alexander while wearing my heavy, clanking captain's regalia. Daniel had already taken the sight of a blacked-up, metal-helmeted Sophie in his stride. The grass was lush and he carried on munching. Alexander was equally, though more unexpectedly, good natured as I levered myself on board from a raised rocky outpost. As a final flourish, I was furnished with a long iron sword, which was fastened around my waist and left to dangle down Alexander's side.

Guides led us back down to the stone bridge and along a tree-lined path and then a narrow road towards the film location. It was further than we expected but finally we wended our way through a wood, feeling as if we were part of *The Lord of the Rings*, and emerged above a clearing, where we could see Red and his entourage waiting below in an historic battle camp scene.

We had to pick our way carefully down a steep, grassy path to the dell. We were roasting in our outfits and the horses were plagued by swarms of flies. They were to be photographed individually, and separately from the other people in the tableau. Red would put it all together technically later.

Sophie's role was to stand on foot with Daniel as he grazed. He was happy to be filmed, only becoming bored after his moment of fame had passed. While waiting for Alexander, he broke free from Sophie and legged it back along the narrow, grassy path to the camp site.

My task was more testing. Mounted on Alexander, we had to stand in the middle of the clearing in front of a large blue screen while Red and his many disciples clicked away endlessly, only breaking off for film extras to rearrange our position and fiddle about with the sword. One particularly enthusiastic production woman fussed around us, repeatedly moving the sword to a different position for better effect.

The session seemed to go on forever and I could feel that Alexander was becoming concerned. His composure had been amazing considering he was hemmed in by people, cameras were flashing and clicking from all angles and the big blue screen loomed over him. To make matters worse, the sword was slipping and rubbing down his flank.

He began twitching and prancing as more adjustments were made and more shots were taken. I sat quietly, whispering reassuringly to him and keeping the reins as loose as I dared. The production crew was oblivious to the danger that was building. If Alexander lost it, people could be knocked over and injured and thousands of pounds worth of photographic equipment wrecked in seconds. He was simmering but the lid was still on.

To his eternal credit he stayed in control and the completed artwork shows a relaxed horse and rider. How the camera can lie!

Red was delighted. But after the session concluded, we got the horses out of the dell as quickly as we could. Waved off by Red and his team, we headed back towards the trailer in the sweltering afternoon heat. Sophie rode Daniel in front and Jenny walked alongside Alexander and I. It was a chance to relax after the challenges of the photo shoot.

We were ambling along, relieved that the day's drama was done, when a man and child appeared leading a donkey towards us.

Daniel immediately began capering and spinning in the narrow, fenced lane. Horses can be terrified by the sight of donkeys and he certainly was. Sophie slid out of the saddle for her own safety as Jenny urged the man to retreat the way he had come. I also dismounted, although Alexander was coping much better with the unwelcome sight.

Daniel continued to pull and prance in the lane. He seemed to have grown about two foot and was snorting like a stallion. Jenny and Sophie, clinging to the bit rings on either side of his bridle, struggled hard to hang on to him. The donkey disappeared from view, back the way it had come. Gingerly, we coaxed a still highly suspicious Daniel past the farm where it lived, and a meadow full of its companions.

When we eventually arrived back home, we turned the horses out in the late afternoon sunshine and went straight to the pub, feeling we had earned every penny of our £200. The horses had coped magnificently with the challenges of the day.

Daniel was now transformed from the scrawny young rebel Jenny first set eyes on at a dealer's yard. Then barely two years old, he was lean and weak with thin matchstick legs and a matted treacle-coloured mane. She named him Daniel after hearing the Elton John song on the car radio as she drove over the hilltops to visit him before he moved with his brother to join The Black Mare at the livery yard.

Mealtimes were then, and still are, the highlight of Daniel's day. In his first months at his new home, he reacted with frenzied greed at the sight of the 'tea trolley', a big blue wheelbarrow piled high with haylage. His ears flattened and he lunged fiercely at his stable door. His blue plastic feed bucket was soon minus its handle and its bottom fissured with a starburst of cracks after he lobbed it skywards.

His tactic of playing extreme football with his snack ball soon attracted complaints. Greedy and impatient, he would stamp on it repeatedly, very hard, then boot it vigorously about his stable. When Jenny went to retrieve it, Daniel bit her savagely on the back.

Checking his feet or trimming the feather on his legs was impossible. He defiantly lifted his front feet, breaking Jenny's nose with his knee, and refused to let anyone near his back legs. Things improved after he lost a titanic battle with the farriers.

In those days, getting Daniel into the washroom was like forcing a stroppy toddler to have a bath. It took four of us. The only way to prevent him lashing out in protest was to wind the hosepipe round his legs until he was rendered virtually immobile in its serpentine coils. When Jenny switched to washing his legs with buckets of warm, soapy water Daniel embraced the experience, although he still managed to bang his head on the hot water tank.

Wendy Wild, a dressage rider and racehorse trainer, was recruited to bring on the young Daniel. She was not massively enthusiastic, describing him as 'a very ordinary little horse', but she set about lunging and long-reining him. He made a blackguard dash for her in his first lesson but she said: 'He only did that once!' On another occasion, he threw a huge tantrum, tripped himself up over the lunge line and lay, legs kicking in rage, in the sand in the school.

Daniel continued to appal 'Aunty Wendy' with his bad behaviour over the years. In her role as steward on Trail Ride days at Craven

Country Ride, she rounded up a riderless Daniel many times as he ran back to the clubhouse after unseating his jockey. But now he was a grown-up nine-year-old and his day as a photographic model proved he was capable of handling the most demanding of situations.

On September 27, 2011, Red's finished tableau featured across a double page of *The Guardian*, with two Daniels appearing in opposite corners of the artwork. Jenny's dad, Alan, rang her at work in great excitement to tell us we were pictured in his favourite newspaper.

That autumn, Jenny, Sophie and I were invited to the preview of Red's exhibition at the Impressions Gallery. We stood with glasses of sparkling wine in front of the huge, imposing artwork and felt very proud when our horses were admired. Surrounded by cultured people in a cosy urban atmosphere, it was strange but uplifting to see Daniel and Alexander glowing in the light of an historic evening camp fire.

Meanwhile, I was preparing for Somerford and the next step was a hunter trial at Camp Hill in North Yorkshire.

Camp Hill has become our favourite venue and it was the perfect place to make our cross-country debut. The course was in one large field and the obstacles were not big but they were varied, asking questions of horse and rider. I entered the 1ft 6ins class, using it as a warm up for the next one. The optimum time required us to trot. Alexander was good as gold, trotting round and obligingly popping over the little jumps.

Until the last fence. It had horseshoes on it that glinted in the sun and Alexander took great exception. He ducked out twice and chucked in a big rear, finally ballooning over it after I let him sniff the offending horseshoes. Jenny was bitterly disappointed. It was her birthday and she had spotted a big box of bright orange rosettes for clear rounds. She was mentally reaching out for one when Alexander dashed her hopes.

Jenny is often teased about her covetous longing for rosettes. It is rooted in her desperate childhood yearning to compete and win prizes, like the girls in the pony stories. Those jolly paperback tales of middle-class equestrian success had illustrations with captions such as: 'I decided to call him Daybreak' and: 'I flew the final fence to win the cup.'

After again narrowly missing out on a clear round ribbon in the early years with The Black Mare at Osbaldeston, Jenny demanded: 'Just give me a rosette!' And they did.

Even today, we treasure every single rosette. They line the beams in the cottage, cover the kitchen mantelpiece and are carefully stored in big plastic boxes. Jenny dreads Keith and Nicola calling round when she is lovingly vacuuming any that have collected cobwebs.

I was chuffed with how settled Alexander was in jumping round the little course and felt it was perfect preparation for the 2ft class, which was my real target. Alexander began the bigger round with some suspicion. The course was completely different from anything he had jumped before, full of strange new obstacles. He came to a stop at the skinny tyres but then jumped it from a standstill and did the same at the next fence, another with glinting horseshoes.

By the time he had jumped the silver barrels, halfway round the course, his confidence was growing and he seemed to have convinced himself that he could do it. He towed me down the hill from the barrels and we did a 'motorbike' turn into a trakehner, which he stood off and flew. We were now starting to work together and when he hesitated at a fence featuring wooden mushrooms in the wood, my firm leg and voice encouraged him over.

Then it was my turn to trust him as he charged into a white picket and log fence. I let him storm over it and he came back under my control to hop over the final little ditch and plastic pole combination. I was thrilled with how well he had gone. We had jumped everything and I was not troubled by the fact that we were given 20 penalties for a single backward step on the approach to the skinny tyres. It had been another good day.

Somerford was now less than three weeks away and my excitement was building. Our performances during the summer had been promising, but Somerford would show if we were going places together or not.

Two days before our departure for Cheshire, Alexander put me in hospital.

I had decided his last bit of fitness training would be a blast up the cross-country field. I went in with Meg Gilchrist, a talented young rider at the livery yard who had expressed an interest in riding Alexander. She has her own horse but wanted to gain experience by riding others. Her mum, Caroline, was not very keen, knowing what Alexander had done to me three months earlier.

'He's really quite laid-back now. You'll see,' I said as we entered the field.

Meg and I agreed to set off together from the bottom of the hill but we had only galloped for two or three strides when Alexander put his head between his knees and bucked. When he bucks he does not stop at one. And they tend to be big.

I was launched and stayed down on the ground as my horse pelted up the hill on his own. I gingerly got to my feet but this time there was to be no walking back to the stables. I could barely put one foot in front of the other because of the stiffness and pain. I couldn't quite pinpoint where it hurt most but I had a terrible aching in my lower back and groin area.

Concerned Ladies seemed to appear from everywhere, among them Alex Brear, a fully trained first aider who immediately took charge and insisted that I stayed lying down. She examined my back and checked that I could move my limbs. Caroline, an optician, checked my eyes while an ambulance was called.

I smiled up at Caroline. 'I guess that blows any chance of Meg riding Alexander?' She didn't need to answer.

I did not want to be lying there waiting for an ambulance but the Ladies were insistent and they were right. Although my head was clear and everything was moving, I was badly shaken up and I knew I was injured. When the ambulance arrived it could not get across the boggy field to reach me so a friend drove the Land Rover to the rescue. I delicately slid myself into the passenger seat and was ferried to the waiting ambulance. It took me to Airedale General Hospital where I was put in a wheelchair and trundled ignominiously into A&E.

When Jenny and Sophie arrived, they couldn't find me. The receptionist assured them I was in the waiting area but I was nowhere to be seen. Then they spotted a pair of feet sticking out from behind a wall. They went round the corner and found me hunched crossly in the wheelchair. It was an amusing sight, though I wasn't finding the experience particularly funny. I felt even less like smiling when I was examined by the doctor.

'I'm sending you for x-rays,' she said. 'There's a possibility you have fractured your pelvis.'

I hadn't expected anything as dramatic as that.

'What on earth am I going to tell my parents?' I thought. They worry about me riding. This would give them good reason to, along with everyone else who cared about me.

But the results of the x-rays brought good news. There was no fracture of the pelvis, or anything else.

While she was waiting at the hospital, Jenny called in on a friend, Gilly Fraser, who was flat out in a back brace on another ward after tumbling from her horse. The ambulances had been calling thick and fast at our yard that week.

My injury turned out to be more embarrassing than serious. I had stretched the ligament between the pelvic and pubic bones. As the days progressed and the bruising came out, Jenny took great delight in telling everyone that *everything* had gone a deep purple!

Though the injury was not serious, it would take time to heal. As far as Somerford was concerned, I could not have timed it any worse. Jenny says I sometimes show off on my racehorse. That blast up the hill was looking like a touch of vanity that had cost me dear.

We discussed the camp and decided that Alexander should go, whether I could ride him or not. Sophie was taking Daniel again and we would decide on my fitness when we were there. This time we had booked into a nearby Travelodge for the two-night stay. We reckoned we were getting a bit old to sleep on the floor of a cold and cramped trailer, although Jenny still managed to fall out of the bath after overdoing the white wine on the first night!

Having arrived at Somerford, I eased myself on to Alexander and managed to walk a shortened version of the farm ride. But it was hard going and my hopes were not high for the next day. David Elms was there and he was already booked to ride Gilly's horse after her fall. Always up for a challenge, he offered to ride Alexander for me.

The next morning, I painfully shuffled on board Alexander and walked to the cross-country field for the first lesson. My tutor was event rider David Llewellyn. I told him about my injury and he suggested I warmed up the horse to see if I could manage. The huge cross-country field, with fences of all shapes and sizes everywhere you looked, was a wondrous sight for Alexander. I trotted him round. It was uncomfortable, but I coped. Then I asked him to canter. With the excitement building inside him, he began to shake his head and body around. The pain ripped through my groin area. I struggled to pull him up and looked across at David.

'You'd better get on him,' I said. And that was the end of my Somerford.

In fairness, I did get a lot out of the camp because I was able to learn about my horse by watching him being ridden under tuition. David rode him well and we have a great set of photos to prove it. David Llewellyn impressed me with how quickly he understood Alexander and how he should be ridden. The pair were put through their paces at cross-country, showjumping and flatwork. Alexander performed well in them all.

It was massively frustrating for me because I had gone there to ride him myself. Sitting on the sidelines and watching someone else do it – however useful that might be – was tough. But I was denied my chance through my own folly. I would have to wait until next year for my big opportunity. At least Alexander had now experienced Somerford. That would serve us well the next time.

There was plenty to work on. David Llewellyn recommended flatwork and lunging. And he noticed that Alexander had a tendency to dangle his front legs when jumping.

'He still looks like a racehorse and he still thinks he's a racehorse,' he said.

But that winter Alexander left his racing past behind and showed us how good he could be in another jumping arena.

22

Back To Black

It would be some time before I competed on Alexander again. Time was needed for my injury to heal: time and patience, something I did not have a lot of.

Ten days after returning from Somerford, I was back on him and taking him for a hack out. Though we only walked, I went too far, too soon, and by the time we got back, the injury was throbbing again. My overenthusiasm had set me back and it was five more weeks before I was back in the saddle.

In mid-September, The Black Mare left the area with Esme. It was time to turn our attention to little Innes. At this stage, neither of us knew exactly what we had brought into our lives. Although classily bred, the new 'baby' was a bouncing, muddy bundle of fluff and Jenny was beginning to wonder what on earth she was going to do with her.

She adored Innes and spent ages just admiring her perfect horse. Jet black from head to foot, the little mare had athletic racehorse legs, a stocky neck and an Irish barrel belly. Barely 15.1

hands, she exuded a bustling joy of living that Jenny worried we could satisfy.

'It's like two people in their fifties having a boisterous child and everyone at the school gates thinking the grandparents have come to collect it,' she said ruefully. But there was no doubt that the young mare was happy. She seemed delighted with everything a big stable yard could offer.

When Jenny bought Innes, she was living a quiet and contented life. She was turned out with mares and other young horses and had never left the security of her birthplace.

To our relief, she settled in with us straight away, embracing the bustle of life at Pilling's. She spent happy days in the mares' big tree-lined pasture at the end of the summer and stared eagerly as horses were ridden past her stable or cantered by in the school as she was led in from the field. It seemed as if she could not wait to grow up and join in. She was sweet natured and loved people and was a delight to be with.

Jenny spoilt Innes with treats and new clothes and blingy accessories. Her headcollar was trimmed with white fur and her smart black grooming brushes had shimmering gold bristles. Friends at the yard chided her about being too soft and doting, telling her Innes must remember her manners. But the youngster's smug and pampered expression as she looked over her stable door showed she had no doubt who was in charge.

When it came to actually doing anything practical with the cosseted little mare, Jenny was far less sure of herself. Innes was to be backed that autumn and we were relying heavily on the help of Sue Chapman and Lorraine Coxon. It was Lorraine who intervened as a nervous Jenny tried to rug Innes for the first time one chilly September evening. Worried that her little girl might be cold, but frightened that the powerful young mare was about to kick off, she could not commit herself to throw her raspberry pink quilted coat over her back.

She was flapping indecisively in the stable when Lorraine came to the rescue, as she had all those months ago when a bed-ridden Alexander was hooked up on his rug rack.

Lorraine purposefully folded Innes's coat and deftly covered her in it as Jenny retreated hastily to the stable door.

'You see?' said Lorraine, with a grin. 'You just need to stay calm and be confident when you are around young horses. Then nothing will go wrong.'

Jenny nodded. She felt rather inadequate and somewhat guilty that Karen and Ian had trusted her to bring on such a beautiful and high-quality creature. But she need not have worried. With Lorraine and Sue around, Innes had the best possible start to life as a potential competition horse. She came on in leaps and bounds and Jenny secretly began to hope that she might one day equal the glory of another Jumbo offspring, Headley Britannia, and win Badminton.

Her only rebellion was both athletic and spectacular. We buckled a leather and webbing surcingle round her middle, to get her used to the feel of wearing a saddle, and let her loose in the high-sided lunging pen. Innes went crackers. She almost bucked herself inside out. Round and round she whizzed, head between her knees, heels flying above our heads.

'Oh my God,' said Jenny. 'Someone's got to get on that. And it isn't going to be me.'

On October 1, 2011, Sue slid expertly on to Innes's back in the stable and the little mare made no objection as Lorraine led her round in the straw. A week later, Innes and Sue were cantering round the lunging pen.

Over the next few weeks, Jenny often arrived at the yard after work to find that Sue had ridden Innes down the lane. The young mare was happy to bustle off on her own, pattering along unshod, with Sue's tiny terrier, Poppy, another bundle of energy, scampering ahead of them. The trio would return just before dusk, The Black Mare blending into the frosty Yorkshire Dales twilight.

By mid-November, Innes was being ridden out alone and in company. She had trotted over poles in the school and jumped a couple of tiny crossbars. It was time to give her the winter off. She would be left to have fun in the field with her friends and get used to the routine of the horse walker.

In the winter months, we arrive in the early evening to tuck our horses in, or brave the chilly floodlit all-weather school to ride or lunge. It is only at weekends, or in the occasional late autumn break, that we get to spend time with our horses in daylight.

The following March, Sue began work with Innes again. She was to be brought on slowly and carefully with the aim of taking part in dressage tests for beginners, clear round showjumping competitions and mini one-day events by the end of the summer season.

Jenny and I had the job of getting her to load and travel in our trailer. We walked her up the ramp, through the trailer and out of the front door several times. But it was not straightforward. We had started the exercise in fine weather, but Innes was not keen, and we felt obliged to press on when she dug her toes in and the skies darkened. She stubbornly planted herself on the ramp, with hailstones bouncing off her head, refusing to take shelter in the trailer. After 20 minutes of coaxing and pulling, we were losing hope. Then Lorraine appeared through the storm on to the wagon park. She waved her coat behind Innes and she obediently walked into the trailer and bounced excitedly out of the other side.

Two days later, she stood quietly while farrier Steven Hardaker fitted her with new back shoes to go with the front ones she had worn since the previous month. Now shod all round and with her glossy summer coat coming through, Innes looked a picture in her black sheepskin numnah, diamanté browband and laced leather reins.

Jenny was so proud of Innes she plucked up the courage to ride her. At first she was very nervous but, after lessons with David Elms, she built her confidence and looked forward to the Saturday training sessions.

Sue was way ahead of her on the little mare, cantering round the school and tackling jumps up to 2ft 3ins high in the showjumping field. She also persuaded a nervous Innes to venture into the deep pool under the willow tree in the cross-country field. The mare leapt in with a great splash, getting water in her ears, and hastily jumped out again.

In May, Innes was taken on her first run with us in the trailer, to a roundabout just along the main road and back. We removed the metal partition and cross-tied her in the middle. Days later, we took her to her first competition, dressage at Crow Wood Equestrian Centre in Lancashire. She loaded well and travelled beautifully.

In Sue's calm and competent hands, she was unfazed by the indoor collecting ring and took a bold jump forward into the new dazzling white competition arena. Her first test score, of 62 per cent, reinforced our belief that she was bursting with talent and would go on to great things.

I had ridden Innes a few times, in the school and down the lane, and had trotted her over a 6in crossbar. I was itching to do more but I was inexperienced with young horses and had to stay patient and let someone who knew what they were doing get on with it.

Anyway, now I was fit again I had my own horse to think about. With our inaugural summer of competing under our belts, my thoughts were turning to the winter, and indoor showjumping. It would soon be my turn to compete at Osbaldeston for the first time. Esme and Sophie had demonstrated the importance of forming a partnership with a horse in order to do well. Would Alexander and I approach that level of understanding?

There had been good signs in recent months. He was becoming more and more settled and content with us. No longer did he peep out from the back of his box. Confidence was building with his contentment. And with that came patterns of behaviour which indicated there was more to him than we had at first thought, an intelligence and perception we had not credited him with. I began to see little touches that took me by surprise and made me smile.

There was the time I casually flung the plastic poo bucket into his stable to skip out the muck. It landed on its side. He craned round to look, then shuffled across and deliberately picked up the bucket in his teeth and plonked it the right way up, as if to say: 'That's how it should be, Dad.'

Another time, when I led him into his stable after riding, he purposefully walked to the washing line at the back, from which we hang his rugs, disappeared head first under his bedtime stable rug, yanked it off the line and stood there with it dangling over him. I took the hint and fastened him up in it. It seemed that his personality was at last fighting to get out.

He was also becoming affectionate. Thoroughbreds are said to give themselves to one person. I was starting to feel I was the one and that lit me up inside. The odd nuzzle here, the long neck bending to see what I was doing there, seemed to indicate that he cared about me. That could only help in building the trust, understanding and team spirit we needed when competing.

And so I went to Osbaldeston, not quite knowing what to expect, but with hope in my heart. Alexander was keen from the word go, peering out from the trailer when we arrived. It was hard to stand him still for me to get on him, but soon we were prancing our way to the hectic bustle of the collecting ring. He was understandably jumpy as horses cantered past him and launched over the practice poles, but I kept calm. I felt he was on the edge and I could see the whites of his eyes as he twisted his head around, but I remembered the important lessons I had learned from Sue Chapman, relaxed my hands and kept him walking forward.

'Don't worry, lad. You're all right with your dad,' I said, gently stroking his neck as a further act of reassurance.

I stayed in control, but our turn could not come soon enough and it was a blessing when we were allowed to head down the tunnel to the arena. Alexander took the pop music, the commentary and the spectators in the grandstand in his stride and he certainly wasn't worried by the fences, which he stood off and sprang over without a second glance. In no time at all we had earned a clear round rosette.

Next was the 65cms class and there were 26 riders entered in it. With only four places up for grabs, I wasn't expecting a rosette. But we qualified for the jump-off with another positive clear round. Alexander was getting the hang of this. He was even going straight into canter when the bell rang for us to start, as if he knew that was the signal to go.

He was enjoying himself, but going about his job in a controlled and professional way. Jenny remarked that while The Black Mare would enthusiastically roll up her sleeves when she entered the arena, Alexander merely straightened his tie.

I took it steady in the jump-off, no silly turns. We were both novices and the target was to get experience and try to go clear. We did. I was pleased as punch when I found that we had gone into fourth position. A place rosette on our first visit was beckoning until a speedy little horse went clear to win and left us agonisingly in fifth.

I wasn't complaining and nor was Jenny when she saw the beautiful pink rosette we had earned for our double clear in the class. We had jumped three clear rounds out of three. Things couldn't get much better. Or could they?

Our second visit was also a success, though we were without a place. But things went drastically wrong on our third trip. For no apparent reason, Alexander launched into a series of rearing fits in the arena. He had to be chased over the first fence in the Clear Round but we still jumped clear. In the first class, he went up in the air when we were halfway round, his antics costing us time faults and a place in the jump-off. I could not explain his behaviour and it was with some anxiety that I set out for our fourth visit to Osbaldeston, on January 22, 2012.

It was a qualifying day for the prestigious national Trailblazers Championships, which would be held over three days in July at Stoneleigh Park in Warwickshire, the former Royal Showground. The Trailblazers finals include special classes for ex-racehorses, run under the RoR (Retraining of Racehorses) banner, an organisation that does fantastic work in helping to give new lives to former racers.

One of the RoR classes was at 75cms, a height we had been jumping that winter. All we needed to do to qualify was jump a double clear round. My heart was in my mouth as we entered the arena for the first round. Would Alexander blow our chance with more inexplicable rearing? Happily he was back to his usual good behaviour and we soared round clear.

Now for the jump-off. I wasn't thinking about winning, or even getting a coveted place. My only thought was to jump a clear round to get us to the Royal Showground. That would be the stuff of dreams. We tackled the jump-off in the same way as any other showjumping round, calm, measured and, above all, steady. No heroics. Just don't touch a pole. The double – two jumps close together – across the centre of the arena worried me. Alexander was inexperienced with doubles and his long stride made them more difficult for him. In the first round we hadn't been very smooth at it, but we had fiddled, and got away with it. It could be our nemesis.

This time we were fluent and jumped it perfectly. The round was going well. Now for the final turn. One last jump. Could we hold it together?

'Steady on lad. Let's keep focused,' I said. Alexander's big orange ears twitched back and forth. Clearly he was listening. We kept our rhythm and popped over the fence. We had done it. I gave him lots of pats down the neck. 'Good lad, well done!'

Unbelievably, we were heading to a national showjumping finals. What's more we had got second place on the day, the first time we had reached such heady heights. That meant us returning to the arena to be presented with a blue rosette, followed by the traditional canter round the outside of the ring. I felt like raising my hat towards the grandstand. This was a day never to be forgotten. I was so proud of Alexander. We were a proper showjumping team now.

Our last Osbaldeston visit of the winter ended in our first elimination when Alexander ran out at the second part of the double. He had seemed to struggle all day. The reason would soon become clear.

When he bucked me off soon after on the gallops at Crow Wood, and Esme, on a weekend visit, noticed he was reacting painfully to her touch, we called in back specialist Angela Brock. She found his back was sore. He must have tweaked it at some point.

Angela looked at the horse in admiration. Then she turned to me.

'He's a really honest horse to have jumped what he has for you with that back.'

But the double at Osbaldeston had been too much. It must have been hurting the poor chap and he was saying: 'I can't do this.' I was annoyed with myself that I hadn't spotted it sooner and spared him pain. Two physiotherapy sessions with Angela sorted him out and by April we were once more blazing a trail to the Trailblazers finals.

This time we were back at Richmond Equestrian Centre, where we had first competed together. Having already qualified for the ex-racehorse class, we now had the chance to do the same in the general 65cms and 75cms classes. The weather was poor and not many competitors turned up. The atmosphere was relaxed and it seemed a great chance for us.

We warmed up in the ordinary 65cms class. We had one fence down but as we were the only entry, Jenny was able to celebrate a first-place red rosette. It joined Alexander's other rosettes on the 'Shelves of Greatness' in our living room, though it didn't count as a win in my eyes because we hadn't beaten anyone.

The course was changed for the Trailblazers round. Alexander – who had been dubbed Ever Ready by David Elms because he is always charged up – came marching into the arena, eager for more jumping.

We cantered into the first fence, which had a spread making it quite wide. It was to be jumped towards the café, with a left turn to the second fence. Alexander's ears were pricked in excitement and he stood off the fence and took a great leap. We sailed through the air, but Alexander's huge jump took us perilously close to the café wall. Before I could react, he shied violently to the right to avoid it. I kept going straight ahead, flew into the wall and bounced off it.

People came dashing up as I lay on the ground. I was shaken but suffered only bruising to my hand, wrist and lower back, and a degree of embarrassment after my first fall in a competition. I was more concerned about my smart, new black showjumping jacket. It was marked with white paint from my impact with the wall but Jenny later managed to sponge most of it off.

Poor me. And poor Alexander. It seemed that no matter how well we did, something always went wrong. We would take a big stride forward, and then another step back. There always seemed to be a mishap lurking just around the corner. And yet, increasingly they were not the fault of the horse.

This latest incident was a completely unlucky accident. The course just hadn't been able to cope with the size of Alexander's enthusiastic big jump. I felt sorry for him. He couldn't help his athleticism, any more than he could help his vulnerability. He was bound to be unnerved by my tumble.

The longer he had been with us, the more secure and settled he had become. Everyone at the yard said there wasn't a bad bone in his body, and it was true. He was the gentlest horse I had ever known. But he was a worrier. It didn't take much to frighten or disturb him, and that often led to drama. All I could do was keep giving him the love and security he needed. The more settled I could get him, the less chance there was of accidents.

Inevitably, my fall was accompanied by a dose of my slapstick behaviour. I was helped from the arena and sat at a table in the café with a bag of frozen peas on my hand to prevent it swelling. As I left, I managed to spill most of the peas on to the floor. A small boy watched fascinated as I tried to pick them up while they bounced and rolled around. Perhaps on a day out with a horsy older sibling, this was the best entertainment he had had so far!

It was another of my regular gaffes, known at the livery yard as 'Steveisms'. One of my best *It'll Be Alright On The Night* moments came after a visit to the dentist for surgery to remove a troublesome root. Feeling sore, and with three stitches in my mouth, I went down to the yard in the cold and dark to prepare the horses for bed. I put Daniel on the horse walker while I mucked him out. When it was time to retrieve him, I waited for his white face to appear, pressed the stop button, took the rugged-up chap off and walked him into his stable, chatting merrily away to him as usual. As I closed the door I was alerted by the hysterical laughter of two Ladies to the fact that something wasn't quite right. A closer look at my beloved little black horse revealed him to be a tall skewbald, who was staring at me in bewilderment while Daniel still revolved on the walker. I quickly swapped them, my embarrassment over-whelming the aching in my mouth.

Another time, I knocked myself out when I clouted my head on Daniel's red metal saddle rack. I came round to find him peering down at me, puzzling as to why I was laid out in the straw. It didn't stop him carrying on with his tea, of course. Nobody came to my rescue. I hadn't been missed, because it takes me so long to muck out!

Then there was the broken finger episode. I rode one-handed all the way back from Craven Country Ride with the little finger of my left hand sticking out at an unnatural angle after it got caught under the saddle and yanked as I jumped a tired Daniel over the hanging log fence. When we finally reached the stables, Ladies ran for cover as I removed my riding glove, fearing the digit would detach itself with it.

It was late Saturday afternoon and I didn't fancy hours of waiting in casualty so one brave Lady dunked my finger in the icy water of the horse trough and then secured it to my other fingers with vet wrap. I went to hospital the next morning.

Nursing my bruises at Richmond, I hadn't given much thought to qualification for Trailblazers. It was natural to assume it had bitten the dust with me. But I was in for a surprise. Despite my crunching fall, and the ridiculously rolling peas, we had qualified for the 65cms finals. A sympathetic event organiser explained that as Alexander was the only horse in the class, and we had success-fully jumped the first fence, we had done enough!

It meant that we now had two classes to compete in at Royal Stoneleigh. I impatiently waited for confirmation to come through the post.

Eventually it did, and my excitement mounted as I flicked through the impressive 36-page professionally produced 'Spillers Trailblazers Championship Finals 2012' programme. There were lists of the sponsors of trophies, sashes and rugs for the cham-pions, and details of the warm-up day, followed by two days of competing. It even declared: 'All spectators and fan clubs free and extremely welcome.'

This really seemed to be the big time. I suggested to my work colleagues they could hire a fan club coach, and I was only half-joking. Then reality kicked in. The reality of how much these championships were going to cost.

One night I sat down and worked it out. Apart from the entry fees for the classes, there was stabling, both for the horse and me, and the diesel to get there and back. It was going to be hundreds of pounds. It was quite simply money I did not have. There would be no Royal Showground this time.

It was not the first time financial insecurity had forced me to make equestrian sacrifices. Sadly, it would not be the last.

23

Money, Money, Money

The ladies in the family would love to be wealthy: to shop lavishly at the big Ride-away equine store near York and to choose the latest colourful fashions from the Joules clothing catalogue. They dream of arriving at shows in one of the 'fuck off' horse wagons that other people own – so-called because everyone else may as well clear off back home when they see their hugely expensive magnificence. Such lorries boast endless gleaming coachwork, rows of ingenious storage lockers containing a myriad of costly equestrian things, and awnings to picnic under with flutes of chilled champagne.

After all my financial problems, I am not bothered about acquiring such obvious trappings of wealth. It is how the other half lives. I have grown used to not being able to afford things: to scrimping and saving, making ends meet and doing without. And anyway, I wouldn't want to be super-rich. It would be nice to be comfortably off, but I am a Yorkshireman. I don't do extravagance. I am always short of money, and always have been. Over-stretched, overdrawn and over budget most of the time.

No matter how much we cut back – Jenny ripped out the heating one freezing January in a sudden New Year cost-cutting drive – it seems to make no difference. Another crisis comes along, in the shape of a big vet bill or the hefty cost of repairing one of our vehicles, to leave us struggling.

When I moved into Jenny's cottage, I brought with me some battered paperback books, a snooker cue and my treasured old record collection. Not a lot to show for 30 years of hard graft. But my parents did warn me that journalism doesn't pay.

When Jenny's marriage ended in her mid-forties, she was able to buy a modest house and a horse. The Black Mare was a necessary extravagance. Jenny had promised her daughter a horse when they began a new life together in the north of England.

The mare arrived with no belongings and, with winter approaching, she needed warm clothing. At that time, Pat Fitton's sister, Sarah, ran an equestrian shop, crammed with things for horse and rider. In the basement was a vast and exciting assortment of second- hand items. Rummaging through this Aladdin's Cave of very reasonably priced treasures, Jenny selected a black English leather bridle, a riding jacket for her daughter, and rugs, saddle cloths and other accessories.

The Black Mare may have been a second hand rose but she was very well catered for at Sarah's tack shop. But then thieves raided the livery yard at dead of night, trundling saddles and bridles across the fields in the big blue wheelbarrows, like Anna Maria, the fleeing rat in Beatrix Potter's *The Tale of Samuel Whiskers*.

Less than two years later, Daniel and Baby joined the family and Jenny began washing up at a hotel in the evenings to pay for their vet bills and upkeep. With The Black Mare doing so well at local shows, Jenny's next ambition was to be able to take her there herself. Being free to choose which events to go to would open up a whole new range of competing possibilities.

She sold her Ford Escort for £400 and bought an elderly but stylish Volvo estate for £500. Next, she ordered a brand new Ifor Williams horse trailer and paid £3,000 for it with her credit card. Not the wisest financial move, but parking the shiny blue trailer at the livery yard and peeling the protective plastic sheeting off the glossy black rubber ramp was a very special moment. Jenny could hardly believe the trailer was hers. She was, for a time, in danger of treasuring it more than the horses!

All went well for a couple of years, except for the day the Volvo appeared to catch fire on the way to a show. Smoke issued from the dashboard and Jenny feared an inferno at any moment. She could not stop with the trailer on a busy and bendy stretch of the A59 and drove on tearfully, expecting us all to be burned to death. Fortunately, the trouble was just a smouldering fuse. It burned itself out and we kept on going.

The end of the road for the Volvo came as it towed The Black Mare on to the showfield at Silsden Riding Club. Black smoke spilled from under the bonnet, billowing around the wagon park. The AA towed it away and The Boss came to our rescue, pulling the mare home with his trusty blue Land Rover. The garage said the Volvo was not worth repairing so it was scrapped, leaving Jenny to mourn the most comfortable car she has ever owned.

The following month saw the arrival of the Land Rover. A shiny pillar box red, it was an exciting birthday present for Jenny, largely funded by her generous dad. Land Rover Defenders are powerful towing machines and we looked forward to venturing further afield. Now we could safely pull the horses over the notoriously steep and twisting Blubberhouses Moor to events at Northallerton and Richmond, as well as heading with confidence down the M6 to Somerford Park.

Unfortunately, the Land Rover turned out to be disastrously unreliable. It drove Jenny to the brink of despair, breaking down continually and costing a fortune to mend. We were forced to have it completely rebuilt with a replacement engine after it blew up on a cold and foggy November day.

But still it broke down, and we threw more money at it. We have spent at least £15,000 keeping it on the road and just about every single working bit has had to be replaced. Now being maintained by a Land Rover expert, it is at last reliable – though we needed a new clutch last summer, fortunately paid for by the AA's breakdown insurance. But the whole experience has taken a heavy toll on our finances.

When Alexander arrived, Jenny reluctantly sold the smart blue horse trailer because he was too tall to fit in it. We bought a bigger green trailer for £2,000. Although considerably older than the blue trailer, it is solid, well maintained and serves us well. A new metal floor was fitted shortly before we bought it and it had just been serviced. The purchase included a matching green tack pack that provides useful and secure storage space at the yard. Our hope is that one day we will be able to afford a small two-horse wagon. The living space would provide shelter on a rainy day and a place to sleep when we go to horse camps.

I keep drawing up new budgets to manage my finances better, while 'Ben at the bank' lends a sympathetic ear to Jenny's latest money woes. The poor chap must despair, after sorting out another loan or re-mortgage on the cottage, when Jenny calls a few months later to tell him there has been 'another disaster'.

We go without holidays and central heating to pay for our horses. When the nights get cold, we get out the hot water bottles, Mole and Badger from *The Wind In The Willows*. Bought more than 20 years ago, they are old friends providing warmth and comfort.

In the winter months, after a day at work in Bradford, we face an hour's commute back to North Yorkshire and two hours' mucking out and bedding down the horses. When we finally get back home, we light the wood-burning stove and sit down with a glass of beer, wine or whisky.

I am still wearing old jodhpurs from my riding school days and the riding boots that Daniel put a dent in before Coniston all those years ago. And half of my clothes are hand downs. The same has gone for the horses over the years, with rugs being passed around between them as they changed size and shape.

Some years ago I quit smoking in order to pay for Daniel's upkeep. I couldn't afford both, so the fags went overnight. That was one of my better decisions. Cigarettes were so expensive. They were costing me around £150 a month – literally money up in smoke – and not doing my health any good. When I met Jenny I was pale, skinny and bowed down with the woes of my world. I am 5ft 11ins tall, but she and Esme, who are several inches shorter, thought I was the same height because I was so slouched. Now I stand tall and straight.

I was ten stone, well underweight, when I was smoking. Now I am a constant 11st 4lbs, about my perfect weight. While some top jockeys have to battle with the scales to keep riding at the top level, I am fortunate in not having to do too much. I can eat well, but I stay slim and wiry. It's a good job, because thoroughbreds are not designed to be weight carriers. Fourteen stone is supposed to be the maximum a rider should be, and no more than 12 stone for competing. If I weighed too much I wouldn't be able to ride Alexander, but as it is he can carry me easily.

Short of time and money, owning and competing horses can seem a tough lifestyle choice. But I just have to look at the array of photographs and rosettes around the cottage to appreciate the happiness it brings us. But there always seems to be a financial mountain to climb and our personal Everest was just around the corner.

24

Waving Goodbye

The part-loan arrangement for Daniel worked very well at first. The lady soon fell for him and loved to spend time with him. She was usually down at the stables three times a week, riding Daniel along the lane and mucking him out immaculately. But as winter approached, things changed. She got a new boss and her working hours were altered. She had less time for riding, managing one day a week at most and sometimes could not make it at all. It meant we were having to do more work in the evenings, just when the cold, dark nights were hitting us. More worryingly, because it was an informal 'pay as you ride' agreement, we were getting much less money from her to put towards Daniel's keep.

With the New Year came a double hammer blow to our financial situation. First, the *Telegraph & Argus* announced a pay freeze for the coming year. Although the previous year we had been awarded a two per cent pay increase, that was the first rise we had had in three years. Yet another pay freeze was going to have implications for our already stretched budget.

At the same time, The Boss, struggling with the same economic demands as everybody else, was forced to put up his prices significantly for day-to-day jobs, such as turning out the horses, bringing them in, and putting them on the walker – all things that people like us, who are at work all day, needed doing. With the cost of straw also going up, the prospects were bleak.

We would have to take action. We were already running just one vehicle. The previous summer my car had reached the end of the road and I had not been able to afford a replacement. We had trimmed our budget in every area we could think of but we were not prepared to get ourselves into debt and risk losing the few things we had. I had learned my lesson the hard way about that. If we were going to ensure we made ends meet, there was now only one thing left to cut back – the horses.

We thought long and hard about our options. Selling was not one of them. We were not in such dire financial straits that one of our precious horses had to be lost to us forever.

However, loaning was another matter. Not the part-loan we already had, that did not have sufficient financial clout, but a full loan agreement where someone would pay for the horse's entire upkeep. They could keep it where they liked, but we would retain ownership. Having decided that, the next question was: 'Who was to be loaned?' That was relatively easily answered.

Jenny and I had found our 'perfect' horses. Innes was everything Jenny wanted – black, part-thoroughbred and Irish. A young version of the recently departed Black Mare. Alexander was the racehorse I had craved since childhood. More important to our thinking process was how our horses would deal with a move to a new home. We had to be sure they would be happy. Alexander had been with us for nearly two years and he had completely changed from a terribly troubled soul to the contented and settled horse he now was. But we were his family and he was dependent upon us. To rip that security away from him could have a disastrous effect. I could not bear the thought of how unhappy that could make him.

Innes was still very young and was dependent on us in a different way because of her tender years. While she would probably have coped somewhere else, it would have been unsettling and confusing for her at a crucial stage in her development. We also felt a duty of care towards her. Ian and Karen had bred her and thought an awful lot about her. They had entrusted us with her upbringing and her future. It didn't feel right to renege on that.

Logic and practicality pointed at Daniel as the one to be loaned. That did not mean we loved him any less than our other two horses. Far from it. But he was a survivor. He was now nine, a mature horse who had found his feet in life.

After his difficult start, he had grown in stature, in every sense of the word, through the years, partly through the toughness of his character and partly through the care and love lavished on him by Jenny, and later me, and also our daughters. He was at peace with the world and able to deal with any little problem it might throw at him. As long as he had a cosy bed, lots of attention and, most importantly, plenty to eat, he was happy.

It was also our intention to cut back on Daniel's competing. He had done incredibly well to achieve what he had in showjumping and cross-country events, considering that he was bred to pull carts rather than jump fences. We wanted him to live a long and happy life and easing back on his jumping to look after his back and legs would help him to do that. A home with someone who just wanted to hack out or ride in the school would suit him fine. So it was Daniel.

Our decision was not made easier by the fact that it was clear cut. Jenny had rescued the unloved Daniel when he was less than two years old and turned him into a happy, healthy horse. They had a unique relationship. I, too, had a special bond with him. He had brought so much into my life. From that moment, which seemed an age ago, when our eyes first met something had clicked. We got on from the word go.

My wobbly riding skills benefited from my partnership with him, lessons often coming the hard way, with me clinging on or falling off him. But the special knack needed to get the best out of Daniel (keep kicking!) provided me with a solid base from which to move on to the different challenge of riding a thoroughbred. Riding Daniel made me a better rider of Alexander.

Considering our limited talents, Daniel and I had some successes to be proud of, none greater or more enjoyable than our two trips round Coniston. The fact that we got on so well played a part in our modest achievements. We had an understanding, if not always trust.

Dan is a huge character, so large you can be tricked into thinking he is human. For a horse, he is remarkably intelligent and perceptive, and he has a wicked sense of humour. There was a merry twinkle in his eye when we played our silly games, like head to head wrestling. Those eyes, so deep and so much going on behind them. And never missing anything. He knows just what you are thinking at any given moment. As he instantly knew when he was to leave us.

I have never known a horse, or a personality, like Dan and I never will. To give that up was going to be so hard. If he was to leave us, even on loan, it would have to be to the right home. Unless we were 100 per cent sure that he would be loved and cared for as much as we loved and cared for him, he would not be going anywhere. And whoever took him would have to be realistic and not too ambitious about what they wanted to do with him. He had to be happy or there would be no deal.

Daniel had a tough start in life and for a long time it seemed to weigh heavily upon him, but after years of love and kindness he had grown into a wonderful family horse.

The perfect solution was for someone local to loan him so that he could stay at our yard or live within easy visiting reach, and we strove for that. But it wasn't there, so we gritted our teeth and placed an advert on the national Horsemart website.

It was a straightforward ad, explaining what Daniel was, and what he wasn't, and supported by a number of all-action photographs showing his finest moments. We were not anticipating a big response. These were tough economic times for many people and, even more significantly, it was January. Who would want to take on a horse in the depths of a long and particularly harsh winter?

But, as with our advert for Baby, the response we got was astonishing. We were inundated by dozens of eager would-be loanees. Emails, text messages and phone calls poured in. Jenny, who had placed the advert, came under constant bombardment for days, fielding enquiries in between trying to do her job. Everyone from ultra-keen teenagers to middle-aged men wanted to know more about Daniel. It became clear that the photos of him leaping enthusiastically over cross-country fences and showjumps had grabbed people's attention.

One woman texted Jenny with more than 20 searching questions and then asked to be reminded which horse it was that she was enquiring about. It is easily done when confronted by rows of photographs on the website, all showing lovely horses in need of a good home.

The vast majority of those who contacted us seemed to be genuine, nice people, all desperate for the chance to love and care for Daniel. At least half a dozen of them deserved serious consideration and I'm sure would have given him the happy home we were seeking for him. But right from the start, one person stood out. Our instincts told us that we should not look further than Katie Gillis.

Katie was the first person to contact us, sending Jenny a detailed and heartfelt email that said everything we wanted to hear. She told us she was 30 years old and had two younger sisters and a mother who were all passionate about horses. The family lived in North Wales and kept their horses at a small livery yard with six stables, in wooded hills with wonderful rides round forest tracks, hacks out along country lanes and up a mountain. Their main activity was hacking out, with fun rides and a few local shows in the summer, when they would also trailer the horses to the beach, just 15 minutes away. There was plenty of land with the stables and the horses were allowed out 24/7, or could be brought inside at any time.

It sounded exactly what we wanted for Daniel. But what really convinced us was the obvious love the family had for their horses. One they had loaned for ten years had recently passed away. Katie wrote: "Losing Connor has left a huge void in our lives as he was a cob who all the family looked after and rode."

Daniel would live with Comet, an Exmoor crossbred pony who 'we have had for 16 years and will stay with us for the rest of his life.' Katie concluded: 'Daniel would indeed have a lot of love and affection if he was in our care.'

We had no doubts about that at all. It was abundantly clear that Katie's family gave their hearts and souls to their horses and would look after them for all of their lives. That might not be necessary, but it was reassuring to know. Katie also sent us photos of the stables, fields and places where they hacked out, as well as pictures of Comet and 'our old boy Connor'.

We invited the family to come to see Daniel and try him out. As far as we were concerned, if they were happy with him, and we were happy with them, they could take him. The following Sunday, they made the two-and-a-half hour journey from Wales. When they were close by they phoned to let us know their arrival was imminent. My nerves were jangling. Part of me hoped they were ringing to say they had changed their minds, and then Daniel could stay with us. But we were committed to our course and I tried to convince myself this was Daniel's big chance.

Minutes later their car pulled up and the family got out. They were everything we had hoped for and more. Katie had brought a friend with her, and one of her sisters, Lucy, and her mother, Ann, who was jolly and kindly and bearing a bag full of Welsh goodies

– cakes, honey, daffodils and a colourful tea towel. It was a lovely, thoughtful gesture and reinforced our feeling that we had made the right choice.

We led them to the big barn to meet Daniel. We had washed and brushed him and he looked a picture. As we all stood in front of his box, the family looking at him for the first time, Daniel shot me an accusing look. Don't ask me how, but he knew right there and then why they were there.

The family had come armed with treats and they had remembered Dan's favourites were Extra Strong mints and bananas. It was a sure-fire way of getting round his suspicious nature. I could see him working his visitors out. I could also see he had come to the same conclusion as us. At the same time, the family had instantly taken to him.

After a few minutes we left Daniel to his haylage and went to the café for breakfast. Then it was time for Katie to don her riding hat and saddle up. Daniel was as good as gold, standing quietly while she got on him, and we all trooped off down the lane. Daniel behaved perfectly, walking out in his usual safe, steady but sprightly way. Katie was delighted. As we walked, we talked to the rest of the family. They were so natural and easy to get on with we felt we had known them for years.

After untacking Daniel, we all went to the pub for lunch, where we passed around more photos and chattered on about him. By the end of the meal, the deal was done. Jenny and I waved the party off, tucked up Daniel for the night, and began to think about life without him. He was going to live far away, not somewhere where we could pop in and see him after work. But we knew he would be in loving hands and the family said we could visit him any time we wanted.

A life in the hills of North Wales should also mean Daniel was plagued less by sweet itch. The complaint, caused by a reaction to flies, ravaged his mane and tail and it was very hard for us to watch as he desperately scratched himself on trees and in his stable throughout the spring and summer months. Although he wore fly rugs and masks to control the condition, and Jenny had tried a whole range of spray, shampoo and ointment remedies, it was still a huge problem that we had never really managed to get on top of. Daniel's change of home to a mountainous area near the coast could be the best cure for a complaint that had often left him in misery between May and October every year.

Katie and her family would return in three weeks to take Daniel to his new home. It was a precious interlude. It was towards the end of February when Daniel left. Waiting for the family to arrive with their trailer was an ordeal, as we shared our last couple of hours with him. Jenny tried to keep her mind occupied by busying herself with tasks. I just had to be with Daniel in his stable. I brushed him endlessly and combed his tail and mane until they were as perfect as they could be. When there was no more brushing and combing to be done, I put my arm round his neck and chatted to him. He put his head down next to mine as I told him he was going on a long holiday with some lovely people who would give him everything he wanted, but if he got bored he could come home at any time. I tried not to show I was upset, but he knew, and he suspected this was to be the day.

His suspicions were confirmed when he caught sight of his travel boots packed inside his yellow feed bucket, an unusual combination. I saw the look of realisation in his eyes and then a sadness. He nudged me gently and I hugged him again. The tears were close now. This was every bit as hard as I thought it would be.

Then the family arrived and they were as lovely as ever and we embraced. There were three of them this time. They went into Daniel's stable to make a fuss of him. His ears went back as he made a final appraisal. Then his ears came forward, his eyes softened and I could see he had accepted them.

Now the time had come we needed to get it over with. Jenny dressed Daniel in his boots and travelling coat. I went to check on something and when I returned to his stable, he wasn't in it. I dashed out of the barn and looked across to the trailer park. Daniel was standing there ready for loading with the ladies all around him. He was gazing in my direction, as if searching for me. I rushed over and patted his neck and then I stepped away. It was time to hand him over. It was for the ladies to load him and take care of him now.

He went into the trailer without too much of a fight. As the back door was secured behind him, I spoke a few words of reassurance. Hearing my voice he craned his neck in a bid to look back at me. And then the trailer started to move, taking Daniel on a journey to a new life. As it turned out of the wagon park we heard a long, shuddering neigh from within. We watched him being hauled up the hill – where he had set out for so many unlikely triumphs – one last time. As he went he let out another bellowing neigh. Daniel was waving goodbye. It was heartbreaking and the tears were now flowing. I peered through them until the trailer, and Daniel, had disappeared from sight. I watched long after he had gone and then slowly turned away and trudged back to the yard.

Two days later, I held my dad's hand at the funeral of Aunty Doreen. It was a tough week.

Our focus now had to be on Alexander and Innes. Painful as it was we knew the decision about Daniel was the right one. Katie and her family would give him the secure financial future we were unable to guarantee at that time. That alone made it right. Friends at the yard had strongly suggested that we should have a written loan agreement to protect our interests and that of the horse. But we argued we did not need one because if we had not trusted Katie and her family implicitly to look after Daniel, he would not have gone with them.

Our instincts about them proved to be bang on. They texted to let us know Daniel had arrived safely in Wales and told us he had already made friends with Comet and was happily tucking into supper in his yellow dish.

The next day they sent an amusing and reassuring message. Daniel had given them a terrible shock when they arrived on the first morning to find him flat out in his stable.

Katie told us: 'We thought "Oh my God! They've had him all those years, and we've had him one day and he's died!"'

It was only when Daniel lifted his head they realised he was just having a contented lie down. It was great to know that he was already so settled he felt able to do that. Let's face it, a big supper and a fluffy bed and Daniel is anybody's!

We are in close contact with Katie and she keeps us regularly posted on what Daniel is doing, along with photos of him at his new home. We were amazed – given his terror of birds when he was younger – to see photos of him grazing with pet peacock, Leggy.

He had also been merrily kicking a football round the field. Then we were told he had acquired a girlfriend. That was another surprise. When he was with us he had always shown a great deal more interest in his tea than in any of the mares.

Far from being upset by the change in his life, Daniel seemed to be inspired by it, embracing new friends and experiences. We were very keen to go and see him but we felt he should be left to settle in and get to know his new family.

It was in June that Jenny, Sophie and I excitedly set out for North Wales. It was a beautiful day and the sea, dotted with little sailing boats, sparkled in the sunshine at Conwy bay. We headed inland, passed the impressive castle walls and rows of pretty cottages decked with bright hanging baskets, and soon reached the agreed meeting place.

It was lovely to meet the family again. Now we couldn't wait to see Daniel. We drove into the woods and pulled up outside the smart American barn that was now his home. As we walked inside, Daniel, who was busily eating, suddenly caught sight of us and did a double take. His ears went half-back in bewilderment and there was clearly some consternation that Mum and Dad had come to take him back.

'Wot do you want?' he seemed to be saying.

It was the reaction we had hoped for. Had he rushed to greet us we would have been worried. The fact that he was concerned we might be there to remove him from his nice new home told us how happy he was. And that was all that mattered. He soon lightened up when he saw the mints, carrots and bananas we had brought.

Daniel looked an absolute picture of health. His black coat was gleaming, he was a fighting weight and his mane had been hogged.

It was like old times as I put my arm round his neck and he playfully headbutted me. As we walked off to look around, Daniel craned his neck and began booting his stable door, a bad habit he had developed with us when he wanted attention, but something he had not done at his new home. It was a good job we were not staying longer, encouraging his naughty ways.

After a while we walked with him to his field. He stood by the gate while I rested my hand on his wither and we patted and stroked him, talked to him and fed him titbits.

He seemed to enjoy his time with us but after a few minutes the audience was over. Daniel turned and confidently strode away across the field, stopping at the top of the slope to look ahead. His neck was arched and he held his head high, like a king observing his domain, before strolling on. This was a very proud and contented horse.

We celebrated by enjoying a meal with the family at their local pancake house and then looking at the big fish, reptiles and otters in the adjoining nature reserve, before taking our leave. It had been a lovely day and it proved how right we were to trust Katie and her family from the moment we first saw them.

Although we still own Daniel, we don't expect him to come back now. He has got the perfect home and he may well spend the rest of his life there. Sadly, Comet has since died, so Daniel will be even more important to the family. We wouldn't dream of taking away the happiness that he and they share together. Katie has always made it clear that we can go and see Daniel at any time and we would like to visit him at least once a year, and perhaps even have a little holiday in the area. Maybe we could take Alexander and Innes for a few days and ride the horses on the beach.

Now, I was building up to a second summer of competition with Alexander and my immediate focus was the Somerford Camp. This time I was determined to get there in one piece.

25

True Colours

Our winter success at Osbaldeston had set us up nicely for the outdoor season and I was itching to get going. I had not made meticulous plans for the months ahead but I hoped to take Alexander back to Camp Hill and build up towards the hunter trials at Craven Country Ride and Coniston later in the year. We would need to keep working on our schooling as I wanted us to tackle some one-day events, combining dressage, showjumping and cross-country riding.

Our first big target was Somerford in May. I hoped it would set us up for the season and tell us more about what we were capable of as a competitive team. I decided Alexander would start his training with a bit of a blast round the all-weather gallops at Crow Wood Equestrian Centre. The theory was to allow him a good stretch in the fresh air after being cooped up for much of the winter, before getting down to serious work.

Hindsight makes things look simple, but looking back it wasn't the smartest decision. I should have taken him on a couple of long hacks out and got a bit of schooling work into him before letting him loose straight on to the gallops. Anyway, I didn't. So when we unloaded him at Crow Wood for his first visit there he was really on his toes.

Crow Wood is one of the most popular and successful competition venues in the area. As well as being an upmarket livery yard, it is an equine teaching centre. That day it was bustling as usual, with smart dressage horses being unloaded on the wagon park for an event in the impressive new indoor arena.

Jenny was concerned about Alexander's edgy excitement and walked with me to the gallops in justified trepidation. The all-weather track at Crow Wood weaves round in a big snaky circle, and it is close to a passing motorway. The thunder of traffic can easily be heard but it is not a distraction for the horses.

I wanted to build up slowly, hoping to settle Alexander, so we walked round the first circuit. He was like a coiled spring but he did as he was told and stayed in walk. We trotted the second circuit and again he behaved himself. Halfway round the third lap, at a straight level bit, I relaxed the reins to allow him to canter. I was expecting him to take off a bit and was ready to react. But as he charged forward he immediately started to buck.

The only way to stop a horse bucking is to keep its head up. Once the front end goes down, the back end comes up and you are in trouble. I tried to keep his head up but Alexander was just too strong, too quick and too powerful. I was fighting a losing battle.

If he stopped at one or two bucks I would have a fair chance of surviving. But once his head goes, literally and metaphorically, he carries on bucking.

I was still there after two but as the third one hit I could feel my lower leg sliding back and I knew the next one would have me. This was a new experience for me, knowing that I was going to fall off Alexander. Usually I was hitting the ground before I realised I had a problem. It was a luxury for me to position myself so that when I did go I landed on the lush soft grass beside the track and was unhurt.

I was cross. Alexander had been naughty and I jogged along the track after him, whip in hand. He had run a hundred yards further on and then stopped, wondering what to do. He was in a strange place and he was bewildered. I think he also regretted losing me. When I had fallen off him before he had cleared off flat out. Now I sensed there was a growing feeling within him that he would rather preserve the partnership. He looked embarrassed and slightly concerned when I caught up with him. Perhaps he was starting to realise he could have more fun with me in the saddle. Maybe, even, he didn't want me to get hurt.

However my troublesome day was not over. I remounted and we left the gallops and rode over to the cross-country course. I thought we could rebuild confidence by pottering around there and jumping a couple of small obstacles. But all the jumps looked sizeable so we went to the water feature. It was very straightforward, just in and out with a small ledge, but the water itself was uninviting. It was murky and Alexander took one look and refused to go near it. I could have cursed. After the setback on the gallops, this was the last thing I needed. I knew I had to try to get him in now, so I held our position and tried to kick him forward. But he was clearly alarmed and kept trying to retreat. As I tried to force him forward again, he reared up and twisted away. I came out of the saddle and over his shoulder and found myself sitting near the edge of the water.

I was still holding the reins but Alexander pulled away and wrenched them from my grasp. This time he did bugger off – through the woods and out of sight. The day was turning into a complete disaster and it was still not over. Where the hell had he gone? The cross-country course winds through woods and open spaces for some distance. He could be flying towards other unsuspecting riders.

Jenny and I plunged on foot down the track into the woods and soon came to a junction. Which way, left or right? We chose left and it proved to be the right decision. A couple of hundred yards further on, the woods opened into a clearing with another water obstacle. Alexander was standing next to it, looking confused. He came to us and I clambered back on. I rode him back to the trailer and we took him home. As preparations for a new season go, this could not have been more of a shambles. I felt foolish.

Sue Chapman was, as ever, there to put things right. She accompanied me on a confidence-building hack out, ending with a controlled gallop up the cross-country field. We were back in there a few days later to practise interval training, which I had not done before. It involves walking and cantering big circles in a timed, structured way, building the horse's fitness and encouraging control. Just what I needed.

Alexander did really well, loping round in a smooth, steady canter, and listening to me when I refused to let him run at the hill. Sue, understanding the need for me to be in charge, was having no nonsense. When an exuberant Alexander cantered beyond the circle, her cross voice drifted on the breeze: 'Stop fucking about!'

I did as I was told and made him get back in line. My new-found authority served me well the next time we went interval training, this time with Lorraine Coxon and her horse Hick'ory. Sue was instructing from the ground. The session was a great success but when Lorraine dismounted, Hick'ory's high spirits got the better of him. He began tugging frantically as she led him round, and despite her desperate efforts to hang on to the reins, he broke free.

Cries of 'Loose horse!' rang out and, out of the corner of my eye, I saw Hick'ory charge past and head for the hill. Naturally, Alexander set off after him. The warning shouts had been just in time. I knew it would be futile, and more dangerous, for me to try to stop Alexander chasing after the other horse. So I sat tight and let him go. But it was vital that I kept control so I yanked him hard once to let him know that he had to go at my pace. Again he listened and we maintained a gentle, rather than a flat out, gallop and that calmed Hick'ory enough for me to steadily reduce Alexander's speed.

Halfway up the hill both horses pulled up and I was able to grab hold of Hick'ory's reins. Jenny was distraught. She was sick of witnessing spills and thought she was about to watch me get killed as the two horses charged off. But the incident taught me a lot about the growing respect Alexander and I had for each other. That I had been able to restrain him, and he had restrained himself, in such circumstances, said much about our progress together.

That feeling was reinforced when I had a jumping lesson with David Elms. He had me tackling figure-of-eight courses and practising keeping in canter while using the corners of the school.

'Now you are working for each other as a team,' he said.

At around this time, David's wife, Joanne, asked me to join a four-strong yard team for a one-off event in Staffordshire, to coincide with the London Olympics. Teams were to travel from all around the country for the competition, which was to be modelled on the Olympic three-day event. We would all do dressage, showjumping and cross-country, with the best three scores to count for the team.

It was a long way to go for one day's competing but it sounded great fun – and there were medals to be won. I was honoured to be asked to be part of the team. It seemed that the improvement in my riding had been noticed. I quickly got hold of my dressage test and started to practise it.

The start of a long, wet summer had already put paid to a couple of early-season events so when the chance came for a cross-country lesson at Craven Country Ride with former international eventer Claire Fitzmaurice, I went for it. Jenny was worried that she would have us jumping big fences but nothing could have been further from the truth. Claire was concerned with teaching our little group of three about control and being in charge, exactly what I had been working on. She had us jumping smaller fences in a steady manner. Alexander had to go at the pace I wanted him to, when I wanted it. Everything went well until almost the end of the lesson.

We were given a line of four uphill fences to jump, still not very big. We popped over the first and then Alexander took off. We hurdled the second at a gallop, ignored the last two and hurtled to the top of the hill, where I managed to pull him up. I knew I would be in trouble. Claire was furious.

'That was a disgrace. Do it again, properly,' she ordered, shouting, 'You shouldn't have a fucking racehorse if you can't fucking stop it!'

Suitably chastened, we cantered down the line of fences in an orderly manner. Despite the rush of blood, Claire was pleased with our work and said I was the most improved pupil. Everything was building nicely for Somerford, now less than three weeks away.

I worked on what I had been taught by Claire and Sue – control and being in charge of the partnership – and in general I had it. We practised on our own in the cross-country field, and though Alexander galloped off at one point, I was quickly able to pull him up and we cantered some perfectly controlled circles, admired by a group of ramblers in the lane. I then made him walk up the hill.

'See, we don't have to charge around all the time to have fun,' I told him. Alexander snorted, as if to say: 'Yes, maybe.'

This time I wasn't going to take any risks after injuring myself two days before Somerford the previous August. In the week before camp, I stayed out of the cross-country field and the pair of us made it to Cheshire, fit and keen to perform.

The preparations for Somerford are painstaking and can take days. You have to get the horse and his tack looking perfect, make sure you have everything you need, check the vehicle and trailer, and do the shopping. I always tramp back from the supermarket with far too many bags containing an amount of food that we are never going to eat. Once you are at camp, eating becomes a side issue.

The first lesson to learn when preparing for Somerford is to make an extensive list. In my case, thanks to Jenny's advice, it is actually two lists, one for me and one for the horse. The secret is to mentally dress yourself from head to foot and write each item down as you go. You have to remember that you will be doing two different disciplines, cross-country and showjumping, and pack for both. You also have to consider the likely weather and take into account the fact that you may get soaked. Plenty of socks and underwear never go amiss.

The horse list is equally extensive. Again, you have to think about what he will wear, as well as his mealtimes and bedtimes. Top of Daniel's 'bucket list', if he was writing it down, would undoubtedly be his feed bowl, with plenty to go in it.

There is always the fear you will forget something important, no matter how many times you check and recheck your lists and examine your baggage. I have only once left something behind, but it was central to the needs of any rider. We were 20 minutes into the journey when it hit me. I didn't have my riding hat. That was disastrous. I would not be allowed to take part without one.

Frantic phone calls were made to our friend Elaine Dawson, travelling a few minutes ahead in her horse wagon. It was thought she was a likely candidate to have a spare hat. She did, and when we reached our destination, I tried it on. Thank God, it fitted me. It was a green velvet hunting hat and looked slightly odd on me, but it did the trick.

The journey itself is quite daunting for someone inexperienced in towing a trailer with horses. Part of it involves travelling for about an hour on the M6, a horribly busy motorway where traffic comes at you from all directions on and off the many junctions around Manchester. There is also the nightmare of the Thelwall

Viaduct, a terrifyingly exposed and huge bridge, arching hundreds of feet above the surrounding countryside. It is a notorious bottleneck and it seems to take forever to get to the safety of the far side.

The first evening at camp is a night of excited anticipation. Everyone is psyching themselves up for the following day, wondering what group they will be in and which teacher they will get. Nervous trips to the stables to check on the horses are frequent. The drink flows steadily but no one is late to bed.

Most people are up with the birds the next morning, bleary-eyed and eager for a hot drink. There are butterflies in the stomach, mixed with a sense of get-up-and-go and a grim determination to do well.

There is a great camaraderie at Somerford. You get to know most people and quickly forge new friendships. You are all in this great adventure together and riders are rooting for everybody else and willing them to succeed. With the sessions split into separate groups, you always have an audience of fellow riders, ready to encourage and support, and keen to see the best horses in action before they take their own turn.

The second evening is a highlight. That is when the professional photographer turns up, armed with individual packs of action shots from that day's cross-country and showjumping sessions. The anticipation builds as the evening draws on, then great excitement erupts at the arrival of the picture lady. There are squeals of delight and gasps of admiration as everyone's photos are passed around the clubhouse. The photographer's professionalism and expertise produces an end result that makes the riders look like a squad of Olympic hopefuls. The snaps capture special moments and are treasured and gazed at for many years to come. You have to buy the full set, despite any good intentions of saving money and purchasing just a select few.

When you are on your horse, you are aware of the photographer but you don't have time to pay her any attention. You are too busy trying to get the riding right to be posing for the camera, although Daniel famously tripped up over the step coming out of the water complex as he proudly stared down the lens.

With the euphoria of photo night behind you, the final day is serious business. That's when you have to really kick on and build on your efforts of the previous day. The instructors push you to the edge of your limits, and your own drive to jump bigger and better overpowers the weariness that starts to take over your body.

Accidents do happen, of course, as they always will around horses, and Somerford camps have had their share of injury and bad-luck stories. Riders returning from hospital, with arms in slings or neck braces on, people stepping in to ride horses for injured friends, even the appearance of the air ambulance, are unsurprising sights. But for nearly everybody, horse camp is a personal triumph and you leave after three hectic days, tired but happy.

I took Alexander round the Farm Ride on my own. I wanted us both to relax before the hard work began the following day. We had a few canters but I opted not to jump. I felt, for once, that I had done everything right. Tomorrow the two of us would face our biggest challenge yet. I felt we were ready for it.

Our instructor was Bianca Bairstow. She is a regular there but had never taught me. I had hoped David Llewellyn, who had understood Alexander so well on his first visit, would be there but

I was happy it was to be Bianca. Many people had said how good a teacher she was, including Esme.

The weather was glorious. It was the only hot week of the summer and I rode in a T-shirt and body protector. Showjumping was first up, which should have been a good way to build our confidence after we had done so well at Osbaldeston. But the session was disappointing. Somerford can be daunting and I was a bundle of nerves. The nerves affected my confidence, which communicated itself to Alexander, putting him on edge. With my confidence went my riding technique. Photos of the session show my lower leg swinging back and my toe pointing down (rather than leg on girth and heel down), along with some wonky right angles in the reins from my elbow to the horse's mouth, instead of a nice straight line.

Alexander, realising all was not well up top, began to worry. The pair of us were fretting and so not working as a team. We had terrible trouble at a tight turn into the double and kept getting it all wrong. My balance in the saddle was not as it should be, which unbalanced my horse, and we knocked a few poles down. It was not a disaster but it had not gone nearly as well as it should have.

I was down in the dumps over lunch, assessing what had gone wrong. But I came out for the afternoon cross-country session full of confidence. I felt that this was our best chance of success and I thought Alexander would enjoy it more. He picked up on my confidence at once and suddenly the team was back. I had got my leg position sorted out and felt secure.

Somerford is about being pushed, and we were. And we rose to the challenge, jumping 3ft-high courses, including logs, tyres, brush fences, a house and, a little reluctantly, a 3ft-wide open ditch. We even led the way by having a go at a challenging solid skinny double.

Dinner tasted better that evening for our performance and we were raring to go the next morning when we went back on the cross-country course. Bianca was pleased with our efforts the previous day. Now it was time to push on.

We set off in fine style around another 3ft course – tyres, a rail fence, two logs, a brush fence and then the house, which we flew. The open ditch was the final obstacle to clear. We approached it steadily, but at the last moment Alexander stopped and ducked out. I came off but landed on my feet. It was my first fall at Somerford, and a harmless one. My second one would be less so.

I got back on and Bianca told me to approach again. We jumped the house, but again Alexander stopped at the ditch. I kept him at the edge as he dug his toes in, and stopped him from turning away. He still refused to jump it, clearly worried by the big open gap.

It became a battle of wills and I had to win it. With Bianca's encouragement, I gave him a couple of slaps down the shoulder with the whip, held him in position and kept squeezing him with my leg.

Then I felt his back end begin to coil and I knew he was going to jump. Suddenly, from a standstill, Alexander launched himself skywards. The leap was huge and there was no way I could sit it. I flew through the air and landed heavily. The recent dry weather meant that the sandy ground around the jumps had become very hard, making the fall a bit of a boneshaker. I bashed my knee, foot and hand and ripped a hole in my jodhpurs, from which blood seeped. As I lay down to recover, Alexander went galloping back to the stables, bucking spectacularly.

I was shaken up but not badly hurt. Jenny wanted me to quit for the day but I knew I had to get back on. After a heavy fall like that you have to get on again straight away or your confidence could be shattered. I sat quietly for ten minutes, remounted and rejoined the group.

To regain my confidence, Bianca asked me to jump a 2ft roll top, a fairly standard and simple jump. But as I turned Alexander into it, I knew something was wrong and he ducked out to the left. Bianca told me to do it again. I wasn't keen and Alexander ducked it again. Bianca asked me to go a third time but I told her it would do more harm than good and I quietly rode away from the group.

I knew the problem was in my head. My confidence had disappeared and taken Alexander's with it. But it was more than that. I had to face the fact that, for the first time as a rider, my nerve – my bottle – had gone. I just hadn't been able to ride Alexander into the fence. I was scared. It was a big thing to have to admit to myself. But that was it, in a word. Scared.

And because I was scared, so was Alexander. That told me two things about him. One, he wasn't the big, fearless steeplechaser-cum-cross-country horse I had thought he was. In fact, he was more fragile and fearful than I could have imagined. It was becoming clear to me why he had failed on the racecourse. He might have all the physical attributes but he didn't have the bottle on his own. He had to get it from his rider.

Secondly, he had come to rely massively on me. If I was confident and positive, so was he. But the moment I wavered, he went to pieces. He needed me to give him the courage and then he could take on pretty much anything.

I had come to Somerford to find out what sort of competitive team we could be. I was learning some very interesting lessons about our relationship. It ran deeper than I had realised and our dependence on each other was startling. If we gave each other the belief, there might be nothing we couldn't achieve. But it was beginning to dawn on me that we had our limits. Maybe we would both be happier if I reduced my goals.

For now, we needed to chill out. We gently cantered around the field, keeping well away from any jumps. This was just what I needed, to relax and feel in control.

After a few minutes I headed to the water complex. We trotted in and out and had a little play. Then I felt able to drop into the water off the littlest ledge. It was only small, but at least we were jumping again.

Finally, I headed to the sunken road. Alexander was hesitant but I rode with more purpose and we jumped in and out. That would do. There was some way to go to reach the confidence levels we had been at, but we had begun the journey. That was all that mattered.

I decided to miss the showjumping session in the afternoon and we set off home early.

I had been left with much to think about. At first I felt very down about the fall and how I had lost my nerve. But I had to put it into perspective. Up until that point, the camp had gone well. We had successfully tackled 3ft courses without hesitation. I had felt chuffed to bits at that stage and I had to hold on to that.

At the end of the day, you go to Somerford to improve. We had done that. But there was no getting away from the fact that the fall and its aftermath had changed things, perhaps forever. Did I really want to jump 3ft and beyond? And for that matter, did Alexander? Right now, I wasn't sure of the answers. What I did know was that my opinion of Alexander had changed. It was suddenly clear to me that he was not Red Rum, or Desert Orchid, or Kauto Star. Had he been, I would never have met him.

No, he was merely a nice, well-bred thoroughbred who had not had the mental strength to race. An athlete, yes. A superstar, no. Someone who needed me to help him through life – definitely. And that was what I wanted to do: to make him happy and to have a bit of fun together along the way.

My mind made up, I did two things when we got back home. I put Alexander's orange 'racing reins' away in a drawer and replaced them with ordinary brown ones. For he was not a racehorse now. And I vowed to Jenny I would never jump higher than 3ft again. She might have guessed my promise would be short-lived.

26

Dreams And Realities

Although I'd had my share of dramatic tumbles from Alexander, not to mention falls from every other horse I had ever ridden, I had never been really badly hurt.

But horse riding, at whatever level, is a risky business, and people do get very seriously injured – or worse.

Ian Olding, a happy-go-lucky professional eventer, was one of the instructors at Somerford Park. He was known as a firm but fair teacher who brought out the best in every pupil. His strong Irish lilt could be heard at every corner of Somerford as he taught. Ian was always central to the fun-packed evening get-togethers in the clubhouse. He was charismatic and popular, with an infectious sense of humour. But his tragic loss while competing was to bring home the perils we all face when we ride.

I was never fortunate enough to be taught by Ian, but I still found myself owing him a debt of gratitude at two Somerford Camps. On photos night in 2007, my first visit, Ian – as always at the heart of everything – had taken the time to admire everybody's pictures. When it came to my turn he was very complimentary, saying how impressive Daniel looked. Of course, Daniel wasn't in the same league as the horses Ian was used to. But it didn't stop him praising us and that meant a lot to me.

He was even kinder to me the following year. I was sleeping on the floor in the clubhouse. Despite a makeshift bed and a sleeping bag, it was cold and uncomfortable. In the evening, I had to wait until everyone had finished drinking before I could go to bed. In the morning, I was disturbed by the early risers making a reviving cup of coffee.

On the first night, Ian, who was staying in a large mobile home next to the clubhouse, was on top form, entertaining us all with his jokes and horse stories. Inevitably, he was among the last to retire for the night, but not before insisting I slept on the relative comfort of a spare sofa in his living room, rather than the cold clubhouse floor. Even then, I was treated to more drink and fascinating equine tales before finally turning in. I was bleary-eyed in the morning but I had learned, like many before me, what a warm and generous man he was.

During the evening, Ian paid tribute to an Irish friend who had recently been killed in an eventing accident. He was asked whether it made him worried for himself. Ian calmly shrugged his shoulders and said: 'Shit happens.'

Less than a year later, we were stunned to hear on the national news that Ian had been killed after suffering a rotational fall while competing at an event in Lincolnshire. His kindness to me and tragically prophetic words made his death more personal. Somerford would never be quite the same.

Rotational falls, when the horse somersaults, are the most dangerous. If the horse lands on the rider they are in very big trouble. Esme survived such an awful fall early in her cross-country career. It happened on her first ride at Coniston, taking part in the Pairs class with a friend. The Pairs is supposed to be a bit of fun at the end of the day and who wins is largely irrelevant. It is the chance to enjoy yourself round the course and gain some experience. A rosette for a place is a nice bonus.

The Black Mare set off in fine style. She was young, enthusiastic and enjoying herself. All went well until she reached the far side of the lake. She got overexcited and too strong and cartwheeled into the second part of a solid wooden double. The crashing fall was on the furthest part of the course and out of sight of most spectators. The pair did not reappear through the trees in front of the imposing Hall. Instead, the next riders were halted as first-aiders and a vet rushed to the scene.

Esme was very fortunate. She suffered cuts to the inside of her mouth and a badly bruised shoulder, but it could have been far worse. The Black Mare was uninjured but bits of grass were being picked out of her fancy metallic silver browband for weeks afterwards.

Horses often have their own style of jumping. Some are exuberant, others cautious. They can be fluent and confident, or hesitant and unsure. A disgruntled Keith once described how his thoroughbred mare had 'jumped like a yak on stilts' at a showjumping competition.

I am very lucky. Though Alexander was bred to be a steeplechaser and has a huge, springy leap, he is also a very safe and careful jumper. While some horses can over-jump, he only jumps as big as he needs to. He is very clever at seeing a stride to a fence and very quick to adjust himself if he happens to be wrong. In that situation, he tends to put in a short stride and 'fiddle', rather than stand off and put in a massive leap.

I have such confidence in Alexander's jumping ability that I tend to leave it to him to make the decisions. He hasn't made a bad call yet. At the end of the day, his sense of self-preservation is very high. In other words, he looks after himself. And if he is looking after himself, he is looking after me.

As our partnership has grown, the understanding and trust between us has blossomed. I am now convinced that he does his very best to keep the pair of us safe. It is a reassuring feeling. My childhood dream, to ride my own racehorse, has become a reality. The thrill of galloping and leaping on him is every bit as good as the dream. But there is a reality that I hadn't anticipated – the depth and warmth of our relationship.

I love all horses. They have such a positive effect on us mere humans. But Alexander is different. There is a subtlety and gentleness about him that sets him apart and brings a special glow to my being. He has changed my life. That's the reality.

27

Heartbreaker

Innes's first trip to Craven Country Ride was planned for a Sunday in late July 2012. Sue was to ride her, with Jenny and Sophie accompanying on foot. The promising young mare would be jumping small logs and paddling in the water complex against the glorious backdrop of rolling Dales countryside, woodland and streams. Innes was coming on in leaps and bounds and we were convinced she would love the whole experience.

She had already been with us to Crow Wood Equestrian Centre and Myerscough College for dressage events. Sue rode her at her first-ever competition at Crow Wood and Jenny plucked up the courage to ride her at Myerscough. She got more than 60 per cent in both her Intro tests and was just out of the ribbons.

Innes won her first three rosettes in the in-hand showing classes at Hanlith Hall Horse Show, near Malham. Jenny proudly pinned her very first prize, a yellow rosette for Best Condition, on to her bridle in the ring for the lap of honour. Inevitably for that dismal summer, it was a rainy and blustery day. As the ribbon was hooked into place, a gust of wind lifted the streamers and one blew in Innes's eye. She backed away but the fluttering thing followed her. Unable to rid herself of the alarming menace, she broke loose, to the understandable dismay of other prize-winners lined up with young horses, and did a lap of honour on her own, with Jenny running round after her.

That evening, Jenny celebrated Innes's success with three glasses of white wine and two double vodkas at the pub. Alex Brear, who helped me when I was bucked off in the cross-country field, was greatly amused when Jenny came wobbling down the hill to the stables, excitedly waving three rosettes. As well as the yellow ribbon, Innes was awarded a blue second-place rosette for Best Part-Thoroughbred and, best of all for Jenny, a rose pink and green rosette with long streamers for coming fourth in the Sports Horse class.

In addition to travelling to dressage and showing classes, Innes was learning to jump at home. She enthusiastically trotted over lines of poles in the school during Jenny's lessons with David Elms. On just her second session in the showjumping field, she leapt a 2ft 6in spread fence with Sue, floating effortlessly over it.

The trip to Craven Country Ride was an opportunity to take Innes on a 15-minute trailer journey with the central metal partition and back bar in place. She had been travelling cross-tied in the middle because she had not taken too well to loading. The trailer was the one thing about her new life that she was uncertain about. She did not want to go in and had jumped about a bit the first time we shut the back door. But she was such a bold and adventurous little horse we were confident we could quickly overcome her fears.

This time, she went into the trailer almost straight away and Sue and Jenny shut the doors. Immediately, Innes panicked. She kicked and crashed about in the confined space, rocking the trailer so hard it pushed the Land Rover along. Jenny was horrified. She had never had any problem with horses once they had gone in a trailer.

After a couple of minutes Innes stopped as suddenly as she had started. She stood quietly, surrounded by pieces of smashed up metal partition. She had a nasty cut on her near hind leg and a deep puncture wound to the inside of her off-hind hock. The backs of her legs were badly scraped, suggesting she had fallen backwards in her frantic struggle to get out.

Concerned Ladies gathered to help as Innes was led limping and bleeding on to the main yard. Pat Fitton's niece, Lucy Cole, was looking after the horses at the stables that morning and took charge of the emergency until the vet arrived. Lucy feared the injury to the off-hind leg was into the joint and stressed the need for urgent medical attention.

Vet Nick Johnson arrived promptly and made a meticulous examination of his patient. He talked the situation through with Jenny, Sophie, Lucy and an anxious cluster of well-wishers, and put a big red bandage on the off-hind leg and a smaller one on the near hind. He gave Innes antibiotics and painkillers and Jenny and Sophie made her comfortable on a deep bed of straw.

I was playing a game of bowls with my son Ben when I heard the shocking news. Stranded without a vehicle I could only wait nervously for developments. Later, I was able to see Innes, and while very concerned about her, I was encouraged by her perkiness.

Nick visited every day but Innes did not progress well. The wound over the hock joint was badly infected and wept yellow gunk. It was a horrible reminder of Alexander's nasty injury almost two years before.

Innes hobbled along on the toe of the badly injured leg. She dragged herself about the box, not able to support any weight on it. Nick injected strong antibiotics into a vein on her neck and managed to clear up the infection. But Innes could still barely walk.

Jenny was terribly distressed. Her beautiful, athletic young mare was a cripple. Just days before, she had been bucking joyously round her large summer meadow. I had seen her mischievous sense of humour early one sunny morning when I went up the field to check on her. Innes was lying down with her friend Cheeky when I hove into sight. The naughty little horse, not wanting to be brought in, scrambled to her feet and ran off up the hill, looking back to see if I was following.

Jenny unfairly blamed herself for the dreadful accident, saying she should not have loaded Innes with the partition in place. Of course, Innes would have had to have been loaded that way some time. It was an accident, the sort of thing that happens with horses. To add to Jenny's grief and misery, it had occurred on her brother's birthday, just nine months after his tragic loss.

We were horrified to see that among the bits of wrecked trailer partition was a sheet of buckled metal with razor-sharp edges. It was a miracle Innes had not sliced her legs to pieces as she thrashed about in a small space with that underneath her feet. The plastic-coated steel back bar, that was fastened behind her, was bent like a banana, and the back door of the trailer was almost kicked through.

On August 3, Nick rang to say he had x-rayed the leg and discovered that a chip of bone was floating in it. Innes must go to hospital for an operation. The next day, we faced up to the nightmare of loading her into the same trailer she had badly injured herself in. Nick came, on what should have been his Saturday off, to sedate her. He also helped to load her.

Jenny was a nervous wreck, with people suggesting Nick sedated her as well as her horse. With Nick's calm authority, and my relaxed encouragement at her head, we coaxed Innes into the trailer and cross-tied her, leaving the front top door open.

Jenny and I then set off anxiously for Hird & Partners at Shelf, the veterinary hospital that Alexander had been treated at in November 2010. I drove slowly and very carefully along the winding upland road. It was a massive relief when we arrived safely, almost exactly an hour later. Innes was settled into a large stable with a deep bed of shavings. There were plenty of other patients in residence, so she would not be lonely.

Equine surgeon Tim Booth, who had operated on Alexander, x-rayed Innes and performed an MRI scan. It revealed a T-shaped fracture into the joint needing surgery to pin the bone together. It was a complex operation which involved inserting a screw into the leg through a small aperture, and there were no guarantees. But Tim was confident he could do it and said success would mean 'a gold standard repair for an athletic recovery'. Without surgery, Innes would quickly develop osteo-arthritis. The young horse would be an invalid, constantly in pain and with no viable future.

On Thursday, August 9, Tim and fellow surgeon Peter Schofield, who had just returned from veterinary duties for the equestrian team at the Olympic Games, operated on Innes.

The day before, after giving the matter anxious thought, Jenny rang Karen Conroy to tell her what had happened to the horse she had bred and entrusted her future with.

'I'm so frightened she won't come through the operation,' Jenny said.

'Don't worry,' Karen replied. 'Her mother has the heart of a lion. She will be the same.'

We could only hope Karen was right and that the feisty little mare had inherited her mother's battling will to win.

Operation day was traumatic. Many people were rooting for Innes and Jenny was literally praying she would come through. We were at work in Bradford, just a few miles from the veterinary hospital, and Jenny sent out positive thoughts to Innes, mentally willing her to survive.

The surgery was in the afternoon list and, as the interminable day dragged on, Jenny waited for the phone to ring. At 4pm, it did. But the call brought unwelcome news. Anaesthetist Sally told her Innes had not yet gone in for her operation. The two busy veterinary surgeons needed to get together for the complex procedure and final assessments were being made. Our longest day just got longer.

We drove to the yard to tend to Alexander. Less than two years ago, we were worried sick about the surgery on his gashed and infected leg. The hospital had done an amazing job on him and I put my faith in the two top surgeons in charge of Innes.

At 7pm, Sally sent a text to say that all was going well in the operating theatre. Innes was still under but not to worry. Half an hour later, Sally rang.

'The operation is over, and it has been a success,' she said.

'Innes is on her feet. Her recovery from the anaesthetic was one of the quickest I have ever seen. She came round, blinked, shook her head and simply got up.'

Sally had then asked the surgeons to leave the room so she could spend quiet time with the little mare, talking to her and checking her thoroughly. We were elated. To me, it was all down to the skill, dedication and expertise of two brilliant equine surgeons. Jenny, who is not normally religious but who had prayed fervently, said: 'There is a God.' There was also the pub. To which we both immediately headed.

The next day, we went straight from work, up the long climb from Bradford city centre to the upland countryside, to visit Innes. She had a giant bandage on and a drip in her neck. She had lost a lot of weight and looked the better for it. She perked up when she saw the apples we had brought.

That Sunday, there was a terrific storm over the hospital while we were there, similar to the one that heralded Innes's arrival at Pilling's almost exactly a year before. The rain was torrential, what Yorkshire folk describe as 'stair-rods'. Water welled up through the floor of the stable block and flowed in a stream down the centre aisle. The sky was black over the hills towards Halifax and lightning cracked across the sinister dark landscape. If it was a celebration of Innes's survival, it was certainly a spectacular one.

We visited Innes after work for the next few days, arguing which was the quickest way through the city centre traffic in the Land Rover. She made extremely good progress and was as bright as a button and full of her old mischief. She nudged off my flat cap, pulled up my coat to groom my back and made a mountain of her bed of fresh shavings.

With Innes most definitely alive and kicking, Jenny presented a thank-you card to the surgeons and all the dedicated hospital staff. It was made from a stunning photo of Innes, taken when she was waiting to go into the arena at Myerscough College by keen amateur photographer Ruth Donnachie, a retired head teacher and a cheerful stalwart for all competitors at our yard. A week after surgery, Innes was discharged from hospital. She let out a big neigh as we towed her down the hill back home to the yard.

Her discharge notes said she could walk a short distance to grass for four weeks, followed by a further six weeks of box rest, building up to longer walks. We were too ambitious with the first walk, taking her round the corner past the café to the car park opposite the all-weather school. It was such a massive treat and relief to see that she was sound that we got carried away, almost literally! Innes leaped about on the rope when she saw a horse in the school and we hastily led her back to her box.

After that, I walked her round in the yard, close to the stables. Jenny was afraid to take her, fearing she might let her go if she kicked off. Innes was calmed first with Sedalin to make sure she was manageable but other livery yard customers learned to beat a hasty retreat when they saw her coming.

On Friday, August 24, we arrived at the yard, looking forward to a bank holiday break from work, to find Innes lame. Nick's boss, David Walmsley, was on call and attended straight away. Innes was hopping when the new, smaller bandage that had replaced the bulkier dressing the day before was removed. There was a terrible unspoken fear that the screw holding the break together had snapped. David reban-daged the leg, to return in the morning with the x-ray equipment. Jenny and I stayed with Innes late into the night. David told us to call him immediately if she began sweating and getting distressed. We tried not to think about what that could mean.

We were back at dawn to find Innes standing at the front of her stable on all four legs. We could scarcely believe it. It was like a miracle. But we couldn't celebrate until we knew the screw was still firmly in place. Nick arrived and we led Innes to Alexander's larger box to be x-rayed. Jenny excitedly told him that Innes was completely sound and the vet filmed the mare marching confidently across the yard.

David joined Nick to assess what they must have initially feared was a catastrophic situation. Many x-rays were taken and emailed to surgeon Tim Booth, who confirmed the screw was intact and not displaced. But it had been a nasty shock and the vets insisted Innes had to stay exactly where she was.

Her sudden, dramatic lameness – and equally sudden full recov-ery – remain a mystery.

With Innes ensconced in Alexander's large loosebox on the main yard, he temporarily moved into a stable round the back. Innes had lots to see from Alexander's box. The horse walker and wash-down slats are just opposite and many horses come past throughout the day on their way out for a hack or to the turnout fields.

It must have been very frustrating for the young horse to see so much equine traffic while she was stuck in a box. When her best friend, a thoroughbred called Poppy, came past on long reins, it all became too much. Innes threw a mighty tantrum, hurling herself round the stable and rushing at the door. Lorraine arrived from next door to settle her, just as she had calmed a stir-crazy Alexander all those months before.

How to safely progress a horse on box rest is always a problem. The 'walk to grass' instruction from the vet can be challenging for many owners. We struggled to keep Innes quiet when taking her on her short walks. She had a wild look in her eyes and would sometimes buck and rear on the lunge line. I was in charge of walking duties and when she went up, I tried to keep calm, ignore it and keep her moving forward. It wasn't a lot different from how I handled Alexander's early tantrums in the school.

Innes seemed to trust me and we fell into a routine. I loved our little walkabouts, even when they were a bit lively. Soon, we were able to put her on the horse walker. Nick was there the first time as she double-barrelled the back of the metal partition with her back legs before settling down.

All seems to be going well, and though it will take time, the surgeon's hope of a 'gold standard repair' looks to be on target.

28

Little Victories

Days after getting back from my ill-fated trip to Somerford, I began the task of rebuilding my shattered confidence. David Elms volunteered his help. His wife, Joanne, also needed to boost her nerve over cross-country fences, so we loaded Alexander and Father Ted in a horse wagon and set off for Craven Country Ride.

I was looking forward to the experience. I still had faith in my horse and I knew David was the ideal person to get me back on track. But as I quietly rode Alexander down to the old water complex for the start of the lesson, my nerves were jangling. What was ringing out very clearly in my head was a serious lack of faith in myself. I trusted my horse, but not me.

We trotted around the grass to warm up and then David asked me to ride into a tiny 1ft log. As we approached the little log I got that same sickly feeling of fear as when I tried to jump the roll top after my fall at Somerford. Alexander instantly picked up on it. He veered away and I let him dance over the edge of the obstacle. I had bottled it again. If I couldn't jump one foot, what hope was there for anything bigger?

David let rip at me. 'That was just rubbish,' he barked. 'Shorten your reins, get your leg on him and make him jump it properly.'

As we came in again, David's voice rang out: 'Leg on and ride him!'

I did as I was told. I felt Alexander twitch to the right. David was still shouting instructions. I squeezed harder with my leg and Alexander straightened up and jumped the little log.

'That's better,' shouted David. 'Keep going. Bring him round and do it again, just the same.'

So I did. And we jumped it again, more fluently. Suddenly, I felt as if a great weight had been lifted from my shoulders. I thought to myself: 'Yes, you can do this.'

We moved to another log, a bit bigger and more gnarled. I kept my leg on and this time Alexander broke into a canter. I kept squeezing and we soared over the bigger log.

'Much, much better,' declared David.

Next we jumped a little course, the two logs followed by a bigger rail fence. We were fluent and positive. The confidence was beginning to flow back into both of us. The rebuilding process had begun.

David had been tough on me. But it was exactly what I needed to make me face up to what I had to do. And it had worked. After that, we tackled the multi bank, the water complex, more logs and a line of jumps, including a brush fence.

Satisfied with the progress of both his pupils, David told Joanne and I we could finish with a course of our own selection in the final field. I picked a brush fence on top of yellow pipes for our final flourish. I fancied the look of it but as we came in to jump, it seemed to grow in size. My negative thoughts went straight down the reins. Feeling my uncertainty, Alexander ducked out to the left.

I had given myself a major problem. We had spent the last hour putting our confidence back together. Now our fragility had brought it crashing down again. I knew I had no alternative but to jump the fence. If I accepted defeat it would undo everything we had achieved in the day. I had to be brave enough to take it on and to give Alexander the courage to do it.

I rode in positively. I felt Alexander's doubts but I overruled them with my determination. He sprang and we were over. I kept him cantering round and approached the big brush again. This time Alexander was more confident. He stood off the fence and gave it some daylight as we went over. It was a very big jump for a novice like me but I kept my leg in the right place and was still rock solid in the saddle as we landed. I felt a rush of emotions – exhilaration, pride and relief.

David strode up. 'When I said you could jump anything, I didn't think it was necessary to tell you not to jump the biggest fence in the field.'

His voice was stern but there was a twinkle in his eye. I had made the wrong decision in my choice of fence but I had put it right with my riding.

'Well done,' David said.

I asked him how high the fence was. He stood next to it and announced: 'Between 3ft 3ins and 3ft 6ins.'

It was the highest I had ever jumped Alexander. So much for my post-Somerford pledge. Jenny had not dared to come with us to watch so I rang her to let her know I was safe and we were heading home. She was then able to relax at the pub in the hot sunshine with a large glass of white wine, waiting for our wagon to drive past.

My confidence restored, the next weekend we went to our first event of the summer at our favourite venue, Camp Hill. It was a mini hunter trial, part of a series running through the summer. I entered the 1ft 6ins and 2ft classes. I wanted us to jump small to start with and gradually build. And despite our ridiculous leap at Craven Country Ride, my clear intent was not to go too high.

The first class required a trot to make the optimum time. Alexander happily went round, skipping over the little jumps, and despite some reluctance at the barrels and the final horseshoes fence, we went clear and finished third, just two seconds outside the winner. We had an hour until the second class and we jumped a clear round in the adjoining showjumping field while we waited.

When it was time to head out on to the cross-country field for the next class the nerves had started to kick in but we started the 17-fence course well. But at the fifth, a pile of tyres between two logs, Alexander determinedly veered off to the right and I had to circle before making him jump it. I was surprised he had taken exception to such a straightforward-looking fence but I suspected he may have caught sight of the next obstacle, an unusual-looking grey castle, which he also ducked away from before we jumped it at the second attempt.

When he did the same thing at the next fence, which had the dreaded horseshoes on it, the round was threatening to turn into a disaster. We were perilously close to elimination. I was bitterly disappointed but determined we would not suffer that ignominy.

The rest of the round proved to me how far I had come as a rider. Despite more uncertainty from Alexander, we jumped the remainder of the course clear. It included a huge leap over a brush fence on top of a hill with a big drop on the other side. I took the marker flag out with my right leg as we soared over. Jenny, watching anxiously for me to come back into view, said she saw a big orange creature suddenly fly over the horizon.

I then had to bring Alexander back to me as he cantered downhill and set him up to jump a 'skinny' fence at the bottom, which he did nicely.

Jenny commented afterwards that Alexander was 'more of a wet dishcloth than a warrior.' I thought that was a bit harsh but he did have doubts about some of the cross-country obstacles that were new to him. I was thrilled with the way I was persuading him to jump them. It was a surprise that I was giving him confidence, rather than the other way round. But we were working for each other.

Two days later, we had another setback. Alexander came in injured from the field, having been kicked at the top of his off foreleg by another horse, no doubt after making a nuisance of himself. He had suffered a deep puncture wound and penicillin was injected directly into the injury to prevent infection before it was closed with eight staples.

Alexander had been lucky. The injury had not gone into the elbow joint, which would have been very bad news. He was confined to walking exercises for a couple of weeks, with no riding, but after that we would be back on track.

It meant that we would have to miss the Elympics team event in Staffordshire. To be honest, I wasn't too worried about that. At first, it was an exciting prospect but it had begun to look challenging. It was a very long way to travel in one day, it would be costly, and another team member had already dropped out. Anyway, my goals had become more modest.

I didn't know which horse had kicked Alexander. It didn't matter. These things happen in the field. But Alexander made his feelings known in a way I found hilarious. He was standing on the yard near to a handsome steel grey Polish-bred horse called Laurus when he very pointedly turned round and stared at his injury, then glared at Laurus as if to say: 'You did that.' They remain the best of friends.

After two weeks, the staples were taken out and Alexander was allowed back out in the field. He nonchalantly ambled off, tried one small buck, a half-hearted roll and settled down to graze. Two days later I rode him down the lane. He was keen, marching along with a brisk, swinging gait, but he was perfectly well behaved.

The next weekend he went to his first dressage event, at Myerscough College, near Preston, but not with me in the saddle. Jenny had planned to take Innes but when the mare had a sore mouth and couldn't be ridden, I offered her Alexander instead. Jenny had not ridden him for two years and was still decidedly wary of him. But her passion for rosettes overcame her fear.

She rode well and Alexander behaved impeccably as they performed two dressage tests, finishing sixth and fourth, and earning two splendid green, orange and blue rosettes.

I was proud of both horse and rider and it was lovely to watch them in the first test. The second one was less enjoyable because I had to call out the test for Jenny while she was riding it. She feared getting confused if she learned two tests, so I stood on the sidelines

and shouted out the instructions. I found it more scary than galloping Alexander at a cross-country fence but I must have done all
right because they finished more than halfway up the order.

The following week, Alexander's injury jinx struck again when he
suffered a cut to the top of his near-hind leg in the field. It was not
deep and he was not lame and I was back riding him within days.

We were gearing up for our second outing of the summer, a
one-day event at Northallerton, with dressage, 2ft showjumping
and cross-country. The previous year, we were unplaced at our first
attempt there. I was determined we would be in the rosettes this
time.

Jenny plaited up Alexander the evening before. There was a
worried look in his eye, possibly because plaiting reminded him of
his racing days. But he relaxed when I rested my head against his
and tickled his nose.

'Just making you look pretty,' I said. Alexander looked down his
long nose at me.

We went with Lorraine and Hick'ory, who were tackling a bigger
class, and Alexander marched confidently into the trailer, glad to
be going on an outing. The horses, who live in adjoining stables,
neighed for each other at the event, even while Alexander was doing
his dressage test. It did not stop us getting a mark of 37.39, smash-
ing through the 40-point barrier for the first time and keeping us
in the hunt for a prize. There were 16 competitors in the class, with
rosettes to tenth place. After the dressage, we were lying eleventh.
It gave us a chance.

I was delighted with our clear round in the showjumping, which
took us up into fourth place. We would have stayed there after

the cross-country, which was a working-hunter course in a small field, had Alexander not dangled his front legs at one of the rustic obstacles and knocked it down.

I was more than happy to settle for eighth place, and a really positive day. We had worked as a team. He had confidently towed me round both jumping phases and our dressage was much improved. Above all, we had both enjoyed ourselves. And that was becoming the theme of our outings.

Our next planned day out ground to a halt on the wagon park. Our trailer was being repaired so we hired The Boss's to take Alexander to an 'Olympic' dressage event. Jenny was to do the Intro class while I tackled our first Preliminary test. Jenny was particularly excited because there were gold, silver and bronze medals to be won as well as diamanté rosettes.

We practised hard all week. On the Saturday, we bathed and plaited Alexander. He looked a picture and was keen for his outing. But when I hitched up the trailer and pulled it forward, one of the wheels locked and refused to turn. All our efforts failed to free it and we were forced to abandon our trip. Jenny, who had been so looking forward to the event, burst into tears. Her mood did not lift when our friends returned later clutching their prizes. Alexander looked completely bewildered as we unfastened his travel boots, took out his plaits and led him out to his field.

The events were now coming thick and fast, despite the relentless wet weather leading to a number of cancellations. Next up was a return to Camp Hill for the mini hunter trial series. I drove us there. I was now confident about towing and it was a bit of a treat for Jenny. It was her birthday and I wanted her to have a better one than last year when an orange rosette was snatched from her grasp by Alexander's rearing wobbly at the glinting horseshoes on the last fence. I gave Jenny the present she was after by winning a turquoise rosette sprinkled with gold stars for fourth place in the first class.

In the 2ft class, we incurred 40 penalty points, half the total of our previous visit. Alexander was keen as mustard when we set off and we bowled along in a good rhythm. But we approached the skinny tyres too quickly and he ducked out to the right. Twenty penalties and any hope of a rosette went out of the window. It was rider error. Knowing he was still uncertain about the skinnys – they are as far as you can get from a big steeplechase fence – I should have brought him back to a trot. When we presented at the fence a second time he took a backward step, costing us another 20 penalties, but then jumped it from a standstill. He then carried on round the rest of the course with the same enthusiasm as before, flying over the castle and jumping our bogey fence, the horseshoes, in fine style.

It was another little victory. We were pulling for each other and starting to get competitive. What's more, we had won our first trophy. Our third and fourth places in the 1ft 6ins class had earned us third overall in the series. It didn't matter a jot about the size of the fences. What meant so much was that we had gone out and competed, achieved success and loved every minute of it. That's what counted now. Having fun, not how big we could jump.

What really made me proud was hearing his name associated with success. No more would he hear 'Adelphi Warrior trails in last,' or 'Adelphi Warrior is pulled up.'

Now it was 'Adelphi Warrior has gone clear,' or 'Adelphi Warrior is placed.' That made me so happy for him. He really deserved that.

A few weeks later, the attractive little engraved glass trophy arrived in the post and took pride of place on The Shelves of Greatness. Jenny created The Shelves of Greatness, a tongue-in-cheek name, on the alcoved bookshelves in a corner of our living room.

For years we have put up our favourite horsy photographs and rosettes in places of prominence around the cottage. But what I was starting to achieve with Alexander was extra special to me, and Jenny was proud of us both. From our troubled start together, Alexander and I had developed a close bond. It was now showing in the relative success of our competing. The little shrine, with its colourful rosettes and photos of us in action, next to a picture of Alexander leaping a fence in his racing days, marks our modest achievements. I frequently gaze at The Shelves with wonder and pride and sometimes have to pinch myself to believe it is me who is riding such a terrific athlete.

The Shelves have become a source of amusement among our friends at the yard, with jokes about them collapsing under the weight of Greatness, as another rosette is added to the collection. For me, they tell a story. A personal one of success against the odds, and of happy times.

Our last event of the summer was back at Northallerton for the same one-day event we finished eighth in the previous month. It was to be our best performance yet. This time there were 22 in the class. I was hoping to improve our finishing position and we got off to a good start by beating our best dressage score with 36.52. Given that when we started out neither of us could be very bothered about schooling, that was quite an achievement.

Again, Alexander's showjumping was immaculate and we were right in the mix going into the cross-country phase. This time it was a 'proper' cross-country course. It included a Derby bank with a little fence on the top; and the Devil's Dyke, where we jumped on to a bank between tall privet hedges, leapt over a roll top and jumped off, before literally galloping out into the country and returning, via a sunken road, to fly the final rustic fence.

Alexander was brilliant at the Derby Bank, carefully popping over the tricky jump on the top and tiptoeing down the steep bank, then switching straight back into canter at the bottom. Our only blemish was to carelessly tip the third fence with our front legs.

I couldn't believe how well we had gone. It was good enough to take fourth place, a huge feather in our caps.

Alexander is becoming totally laid-back about his competing. He munches his haylage in the trailer before the start, but once the saddle and bridle are on, it is like switching on a light and he goes out and does his job calmly and professionally. Once he has finished, the light goes back off and he nonchalantly stands and sunbathes and eats grass before it is time to go home. Our competition days are an absolute pleasure, not just for me, he clearly loves them too.

Karen Conroy made a telling remark when she said Alexander was happy because he was within his comfort zone. He might have been more than capable of jumping 4ft 6ins steeplechase fences but that didn't mean he enjoyed it, especially if he was being buffeted by other horses in a race. Now there is no pressure.

Every time we competed last summer, we got a place and a rosette. Little victories marking a major personal triumph. Each small step together represented a giant leap for the two of us. We have come a long way together, and not just competitively. We have come to depend on one another and to give each other strength and security.

Alexander still doesn't give much away, but more of his personality is coming out and he is a lot brighter than I at first gave him credit for. He keeps surprising me. One day I was standing just inside his stable door, getting ready to take off his rug. As part of our daily one-way chit chat, I said: 'I'll need some room if I'm going to undo this.' Instantly, Alexander took two steps back. I hadn't asked him to do anything. He just understood what was needed.

I smiled up at him. 'You're a clever bugger, aren't you!'

He let out a big sigh, as if to say: 'Of course I am.'

I have had a lot of valuable help on this exciting journey, not just from Sue Chapman, David Elms, and, of course, Jenny, but from people like Sue Dinsdale. She takes Alexander on a long hack out once a week, with her friend Linda Whitton who rides Star, while we are at work, and then mucks him out.

It takes a lot of pressure off me to have him exercised and looked after. Sue is used to riding ex-racehorses and is unfazed by Alexander. She has struck up a bond with him and, like me, fell for his gentle personality.

She said to me one day: 'Sometimes you just click with a horse. I really love him.' I know exactly what she means.

Alexander's sweet nature has really come to the fore. When I crouch down to fasten the front straps on his rug, he stops eating his hay and rests his chin on my back – like his mother used to do in her quieter moments. He is always poking his long nose towards me to see what I am doing, and he is very polite when asking for mints. And it only takes a quiet word and a light touch of his neck for him to wait patiently while his haynet is tied up before he eats it. His stable manners are impeccable. I can muck out around him without any trouble and he doesn't mind me working in his box while he eats.

Even when he gets to run on grass, his behaviour cannot be faulted. He has never bolted, he won't go faster than I want him to and he always listens when I ask him to slow down. The falls I have had from him have mostly been my fault. There haven't been many, considering what we have achieved together, and they are getting fewer. I have only once broken anything and that was when I fractured my little finger when I caught it under the saddle while jumping Daniel.

The new restrained Alexander means we have become popular riding partners with others at the livery yard. At first nobody wanted to get too close to us. We were too wild and unpredictable and we were left to go our own way. Now, young ladies queue up to ride out with us. It's not bad for the middle-aged male ego!

Jess Jackson, whose palomino mare, Kira, has caught Alexander's eye, fondly dubbed him 'The Creature' because of his striking athleticism. She originally admired him from a distance but now regularly demands our company on her hacks out and is seeking to make it a foursome in the Pairs at Coniston. That will have to be next autumn. Coniston Hunter Trials became one of the many casualties of the non-stop rain of 2012. It had been my end-of-season target, the big challenge to cap off the year. I will be aiming to try to do well there next year. It will suit Alexander down to the ground and, in my eyes, it is still the top place to go and do the business.

The plan is for Keith to take Alexander to the prestigious Skipton Horse Trials in 2013. It would make me so proud to watch them go round. Skipton's fences look too big for me, at least that's how I see it at the moment. But Alexander deserves his chance. He is Keith's type of horse and I think he was hoping he might get asked to do the honours!

Of course, there is little Innes waiting in the wings too. We are keeping our fingers crossed, and there is still some way to go, but she is recovering well. In a few months, we hope to be riding her again. We remain confident that she will give us lots of fun and success as an event horse. A friend of ours called to see her recently. He predicted she would soon be 'leaping at the moon' and we believe him.

Racehorses have so much to give, and so much to do, when their careers end. Recent steeplechasing greats such as Denman, who is hunting and team chasing, and both Kauto Star and Grand National winner Neptune Collonges, who have taken up dressage, are enjoying their new challenges.

Alexander loves his new life of showjumping and little one-day events. But life with him is about much more than going out to compete. It is about what we give to each other and what we have done for each other. The happiness and security we now share.

I have come a long way in my life in the last few years. Much of it is due to what I have been given by Jenny and the horses, in particular a mischievous gypsy trotter and a failed racehorse. Alexander and I have had our ups and downs. I am mostly to blame for my accidents, trying to do too much too soon. You have to give ex-racers time to adapt to their new lives and yourself time to adapt to them. They are different. But if you remember that, you will get your rewards.

The success and the joy Alexander and I now have together cannot be measured. What he has brought to me demonstrates how much ex-racehorses have to offer ordinary folk. They can be wonderful companions, in competition and in life, and they can make dreams come true. Alexander certainly has for me. He may have been a long way from winning on the racecourse. But we are both winners now because we have brought each other happiness. And that is the biggest prize of all.

Acknowledgements

My journey with horses has been eventful and fulfilling. I could not have made it without a number of people. My special thanks go to Ian and Karen Conroy – for had they not given Alexander two chances in life, I would never have met him.

Particular mention should also be made of Sue Chapman and David Elms for their skills and understanding in teaching me how to ride an ex-racehorse; and Keith Rosier and Nicola Binns, whose loyalty and support has given me so much riding confidence.

Thanks, too, to all those who played a part in Alexander's early life and were good enough to tell me about it, in particular Norman Babbage and his family; and to Carol and Bob Bridgestock, without whom the book may never have been completed.

I will forever be thankful for the love and support of my mum and dad; my children, Emma, Sophie and Ben; and Jenny, who gave me a fantastic new life.

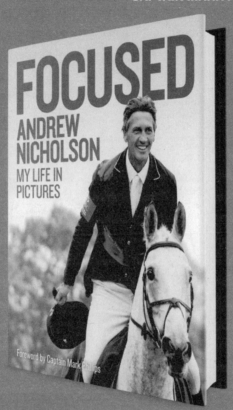